FASHION FORWARD 3

LISE Publishing

Box 2198
St. Marys, Ontario, N4X 1A1
lisepublishing@mail.com

Copyright© 2016 by Shirley Lise

All rights reserved. This book is protected by copyright laws. No part of it may be copied or reproduced or transmitted by any means without the written permission of the author.

Interior & Cover Design
by Shirley Lise

ISBN 13: 978-1535118620

ISBN 10: 1535118628

Manufactured in
the United States of America

THE ADULT COLORING BOOK ADVENTURE

Yes, we all know children love to color. We appreciate the opportunity for creative expression as our child definitively picks out the exact colored pencil she will use. We recognize the effectiveness of an outline that challenges her to color within its lines and develop motor skills. Thus, the coloring book has always been part and parcel of childhood experience.

But there are more benefits to expressing oneself through the media of coloring. Coloring gives a sense of pleasure as the subject takes on new dimensions as color is applied. Coloring is soothing. It is also fulfilling, providing a sense of accomplishment.

With the benefits of coloring and coloring books, why restrict the activity to children? Why not extend it to adults? That is exactly what the production of an ADULT COLORING BOOK intends to do.

Do you have a creative passion, a desire to express what is inside you? There are many ways to do this, such as painting, drawing, scrapbooking, needlework, just to name a few less adventurous means, and other more adventurous such as sewing, upholstering, building, and many more. All these bring out the artist in us. Many of these take time and effort to organize and present a challenge to fit into our already busy schedules. Coloring solves this problem.

A coloring book is a quicker, more accessible and convenient option to other methods of expression as well as a less-expensive one. When you have a few minutes to unwind, just pull out your coloring book and pencil crayons and you are good to go.

Coloring is relaxing, and who does not need to relax and ward off stress from time to time? Why not take advantage of this easy help to release tension, and just as a child, experience coloring's soothing quality.

And what about the sense of fulfilment created when a page is finally colored? You can then indulge in the reward of your efforts, the finished product. If you are brave enough, you can frame it and pin it up for display on a wall in your home for continued viewing, or post it publically for others to see and enjoy as well.

The ADULT COLORING BOOK has many benefits to offer including a personal journal to jot down your thoughts as you color. I hope that as you engage in the activity provided by the pages of FASHION FORWARD 3, the third in a series of fashion adult coloring books, you will experience them all!

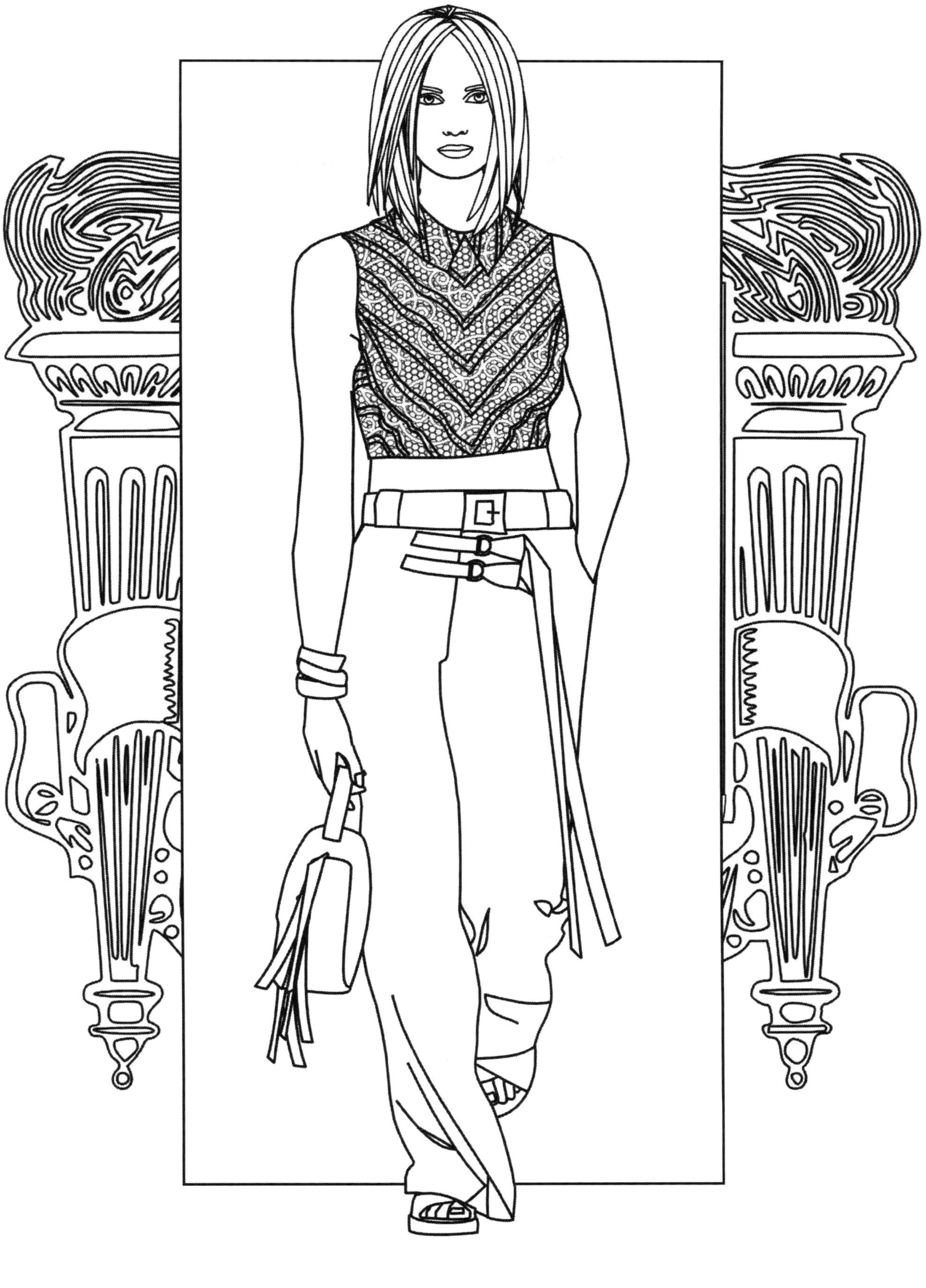

FASHION NOTES

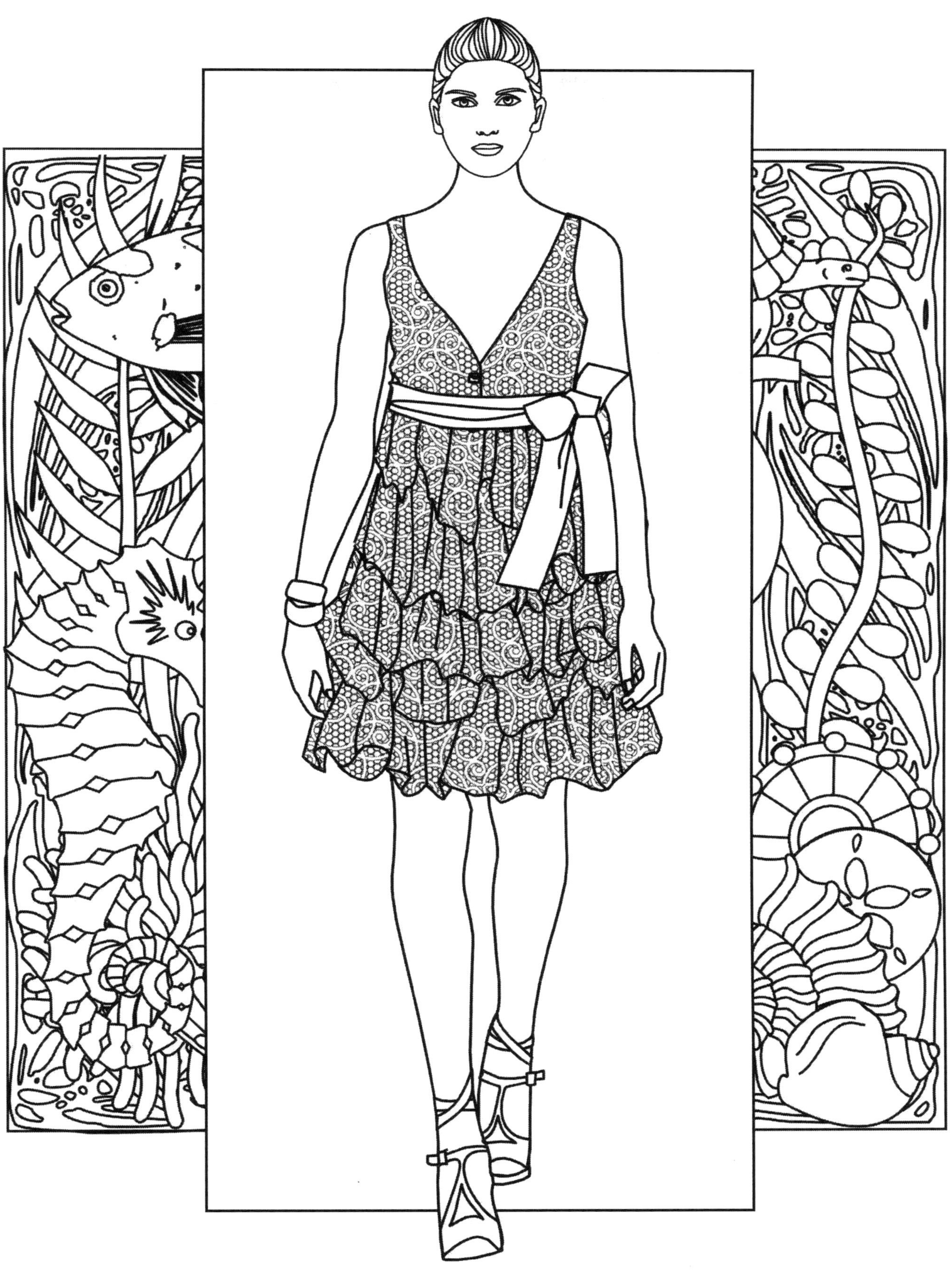

FASHION NOTES

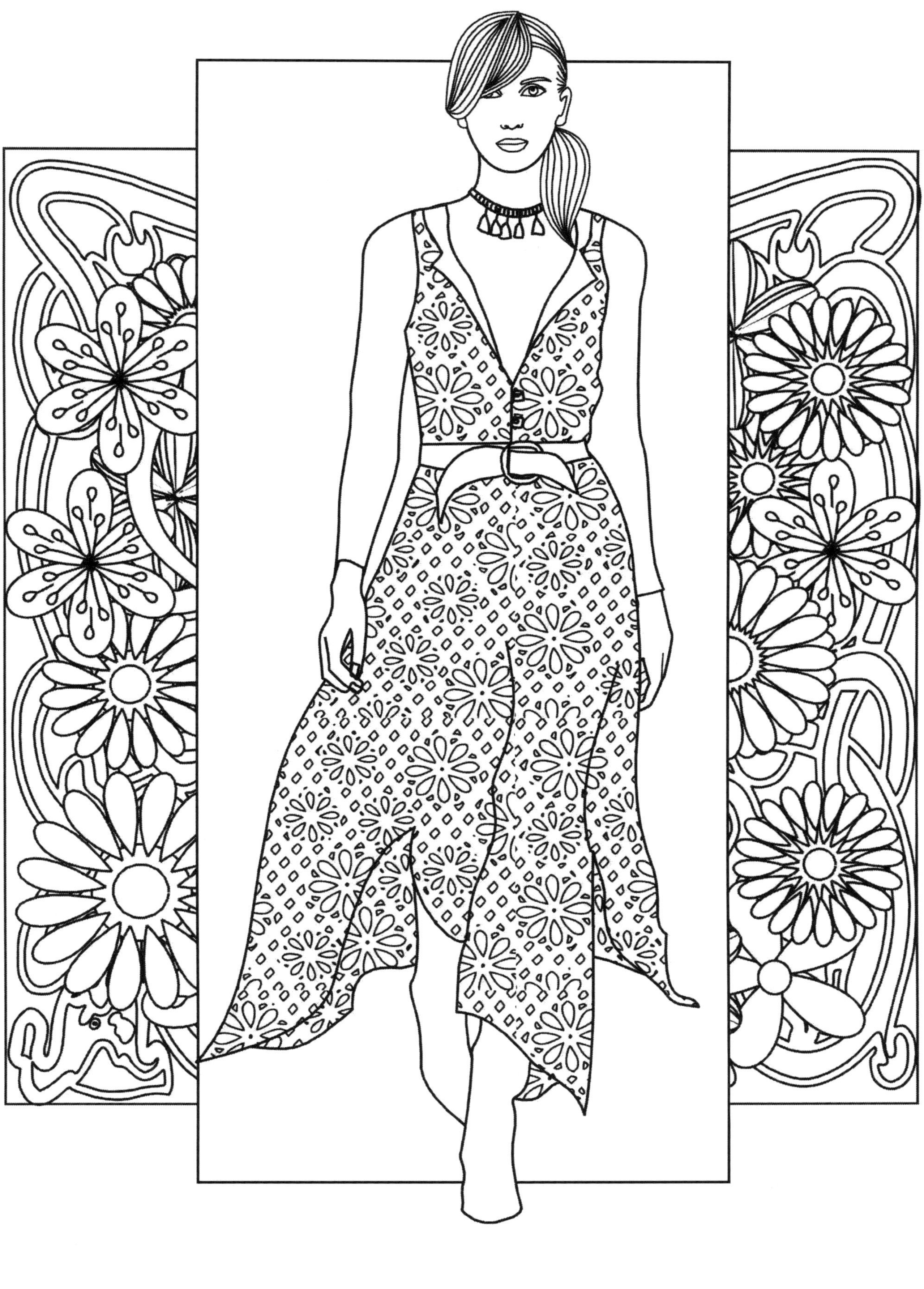

FASHION NOTES

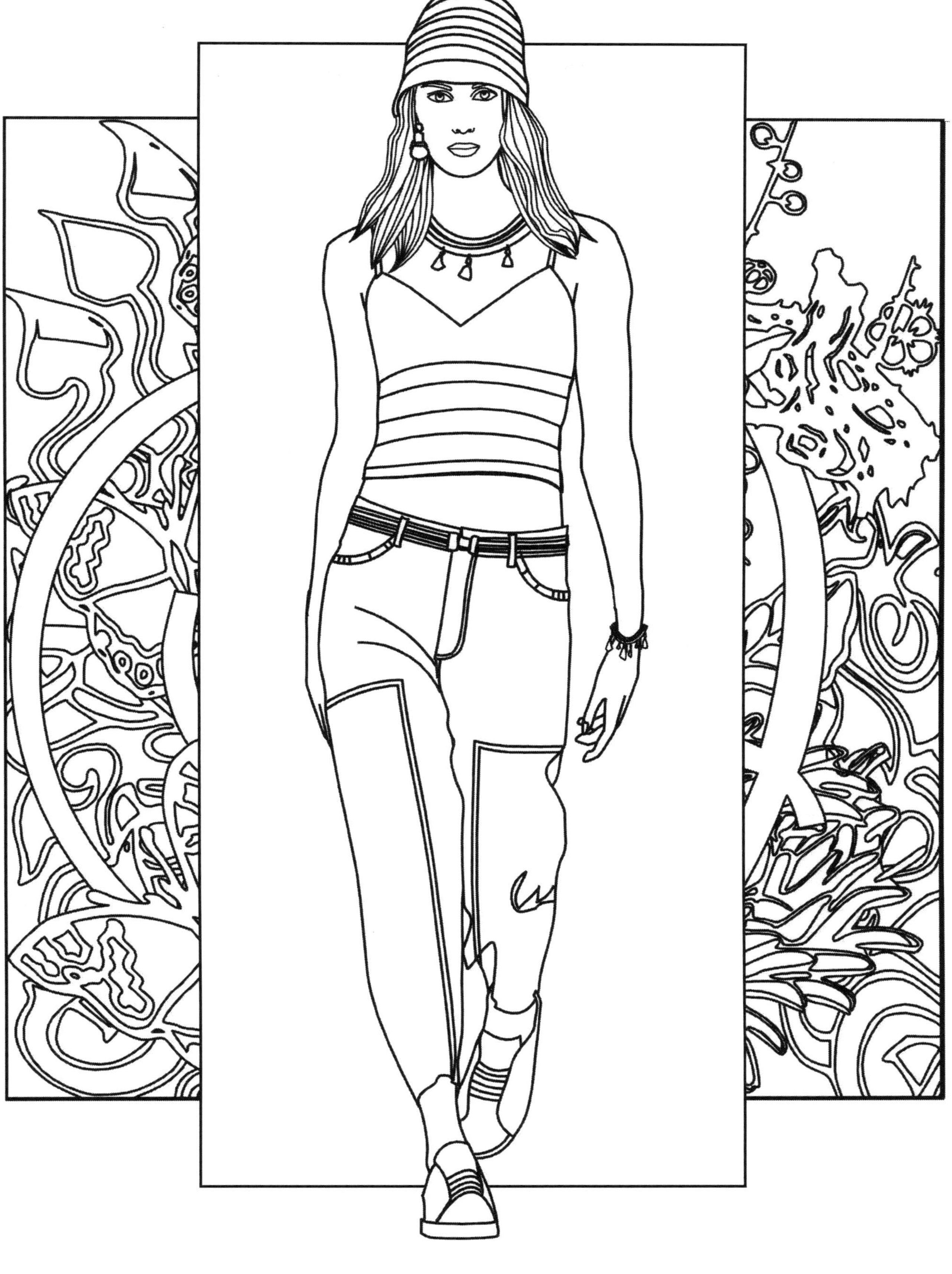

FASHION NOTES

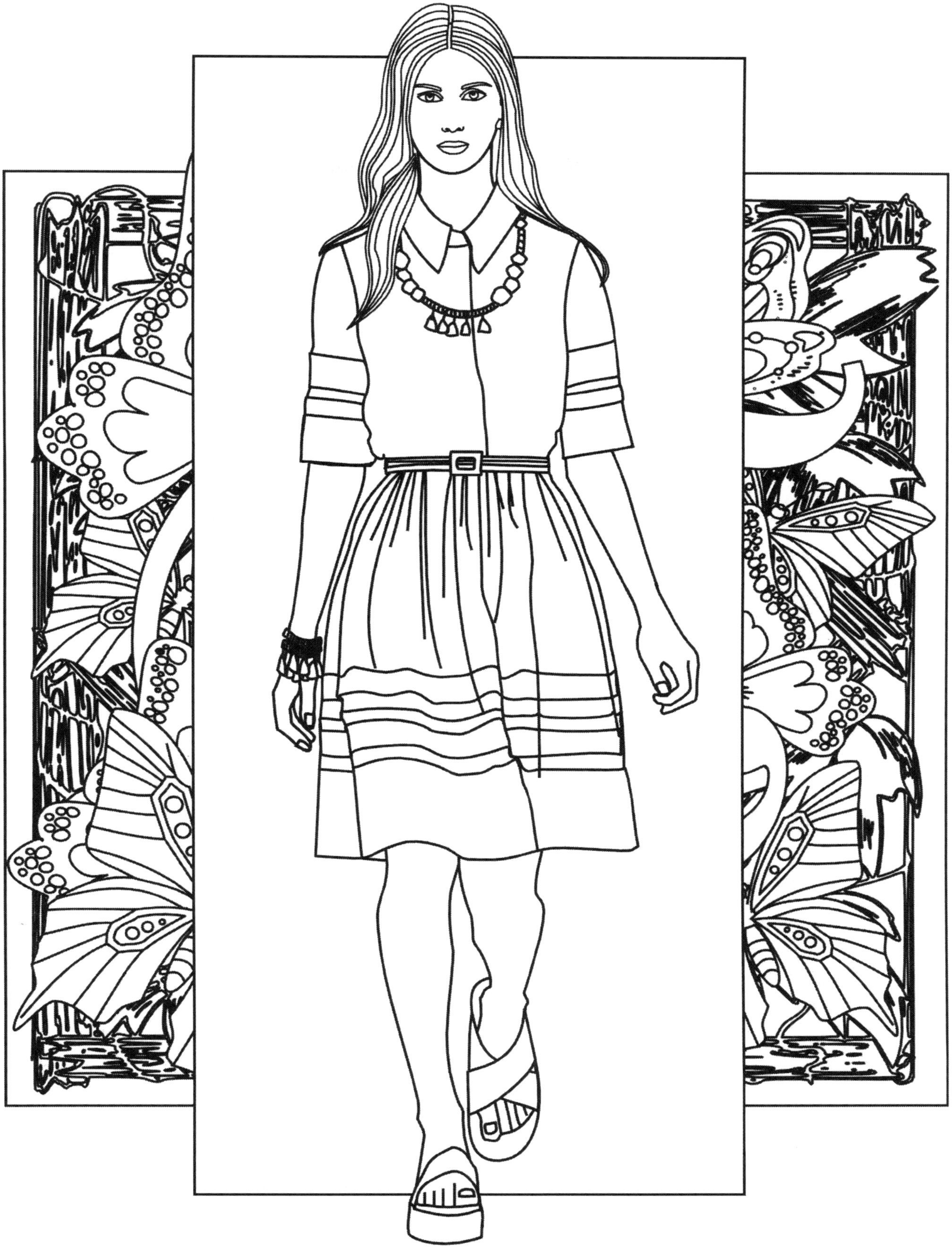

FASHION NOTES

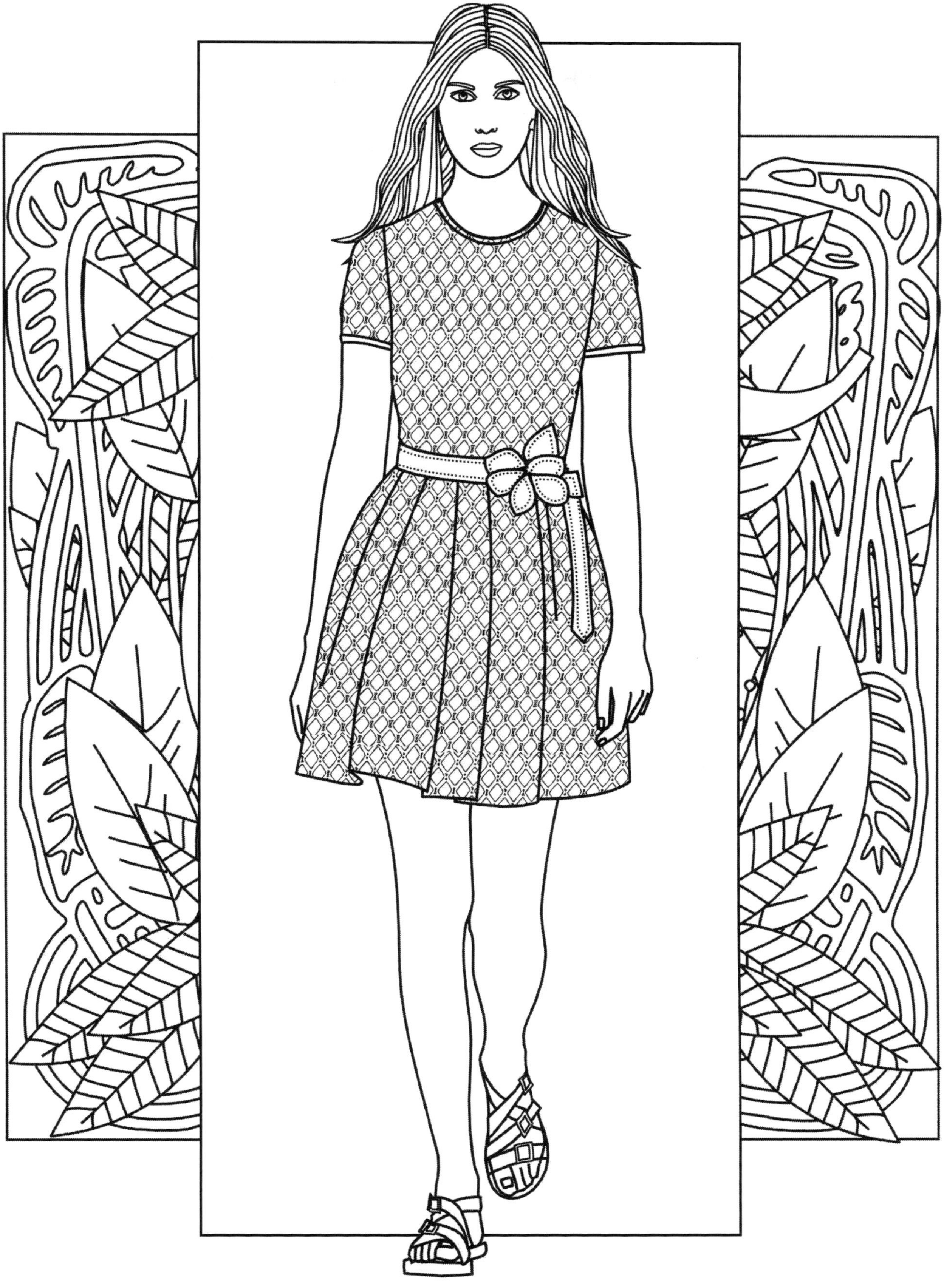

FASHION NOTES

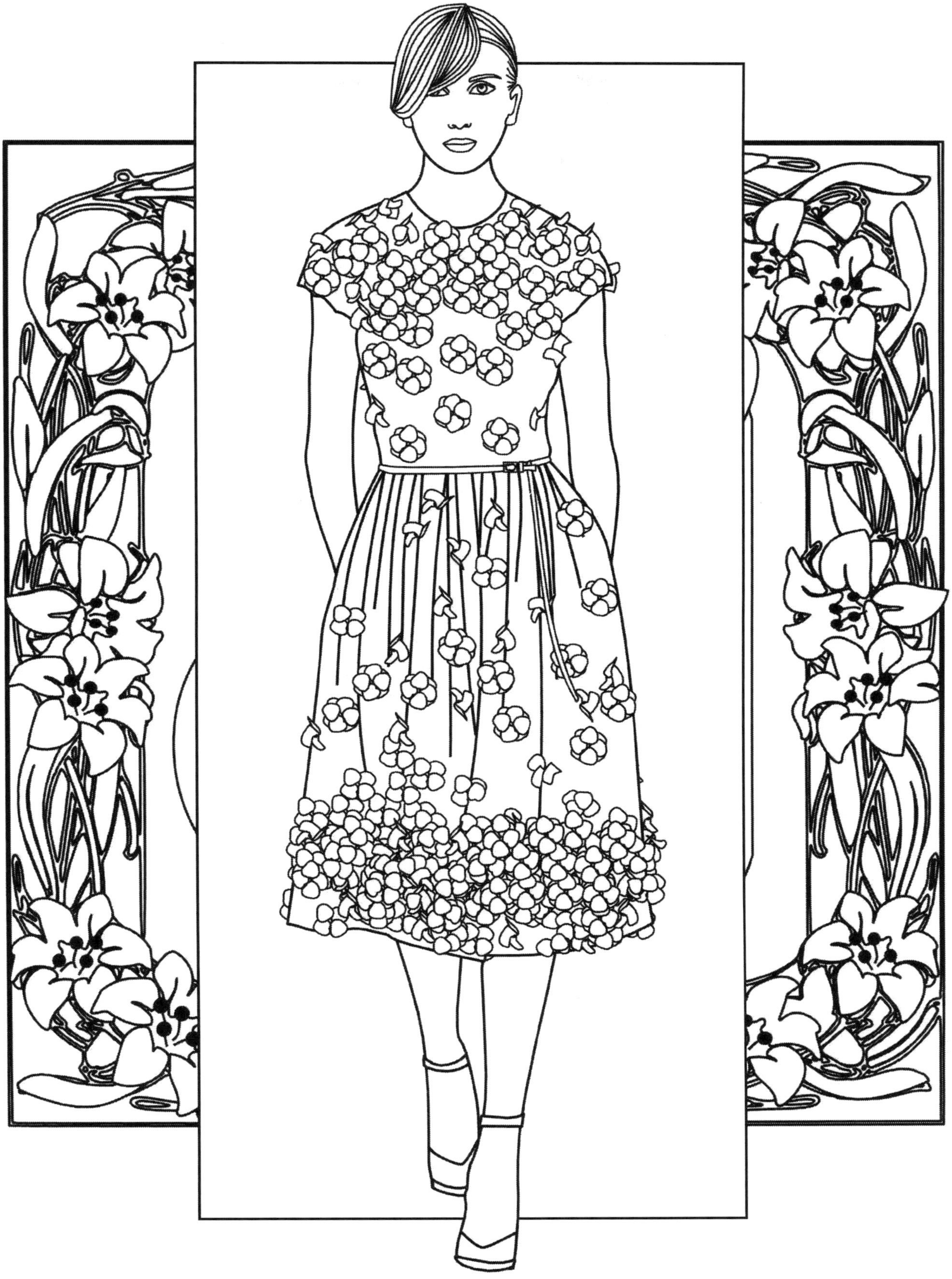

FASHION NOTES

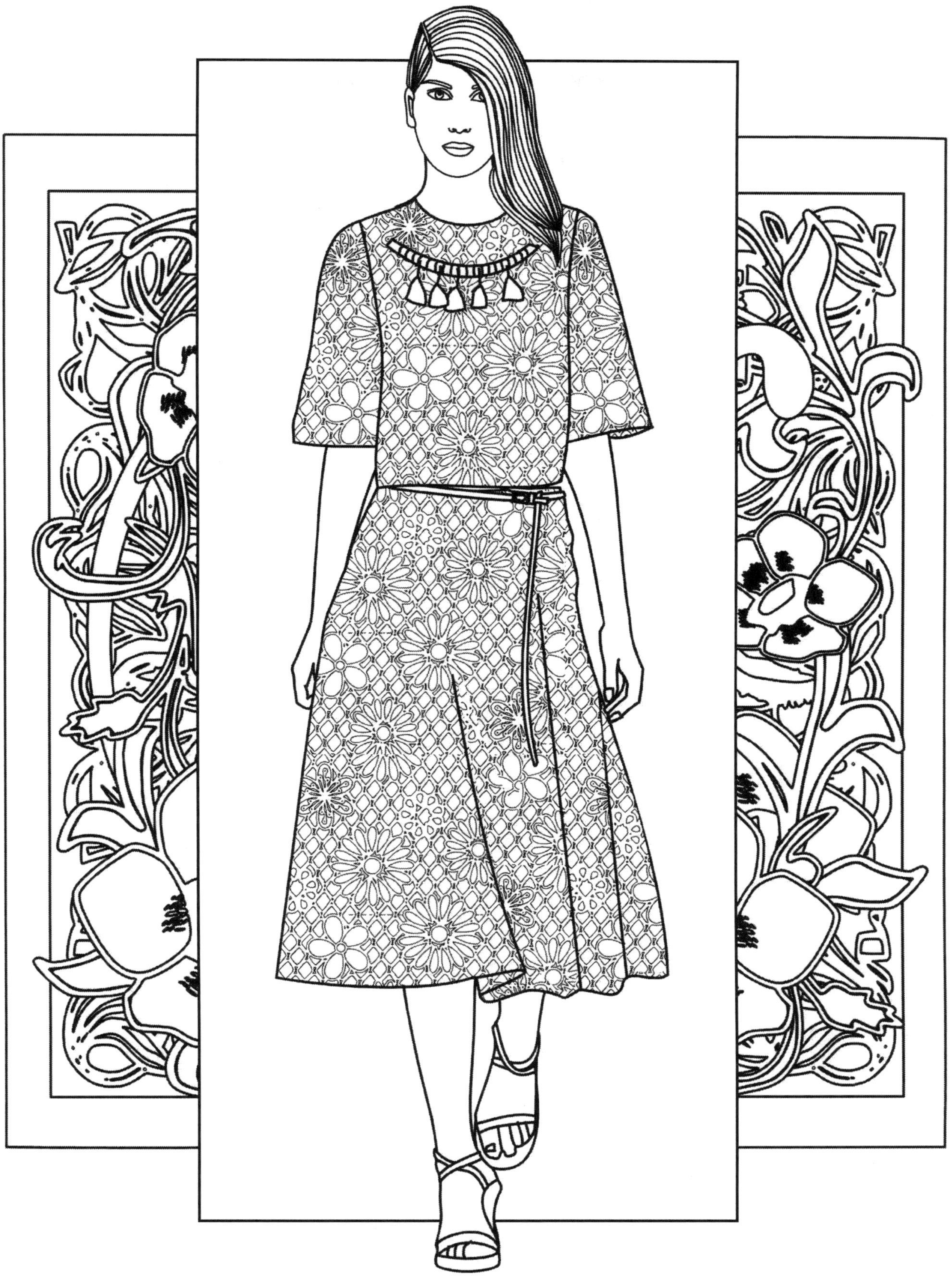

FASHION NOTES

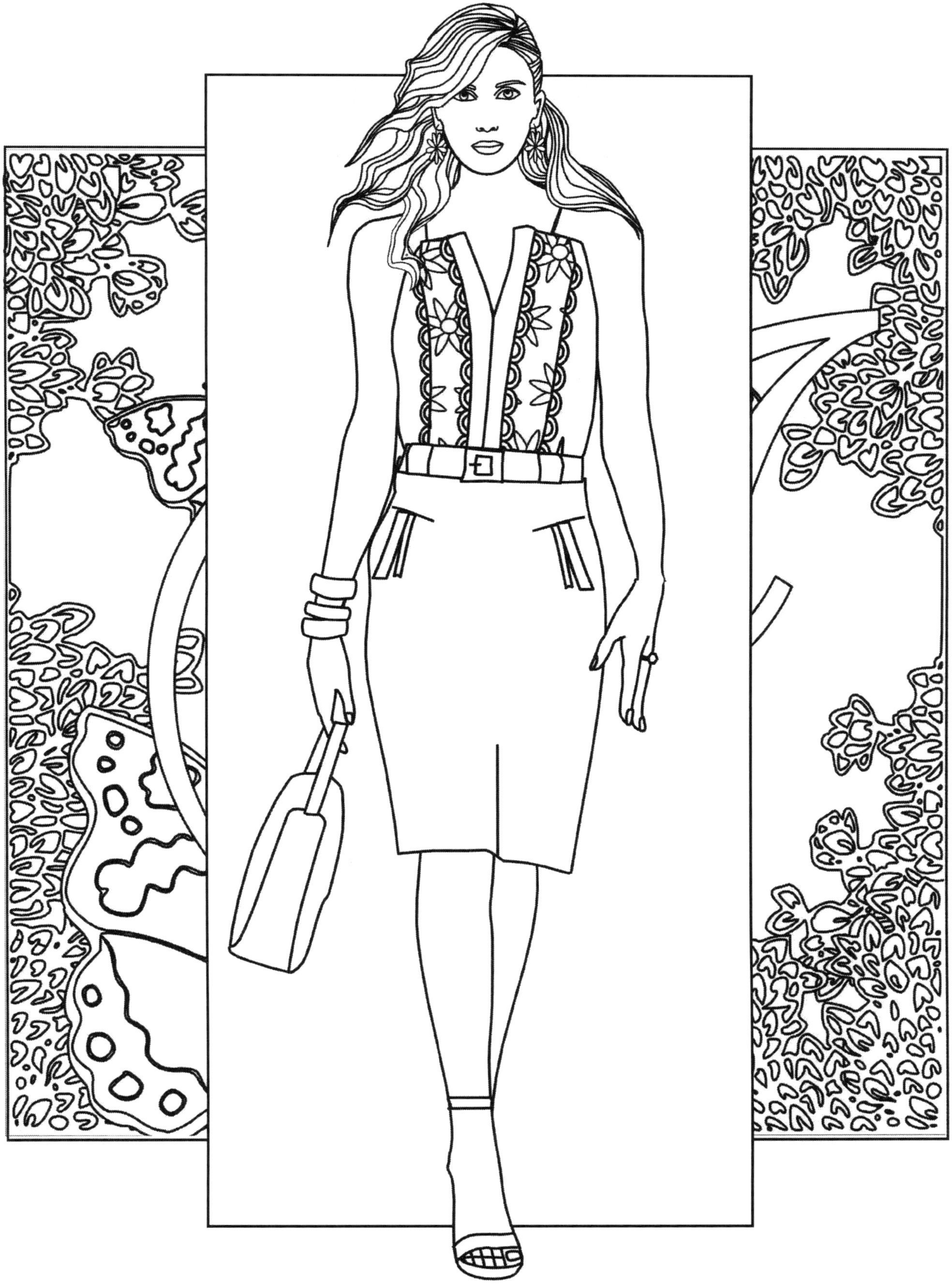

FASHION NOTES

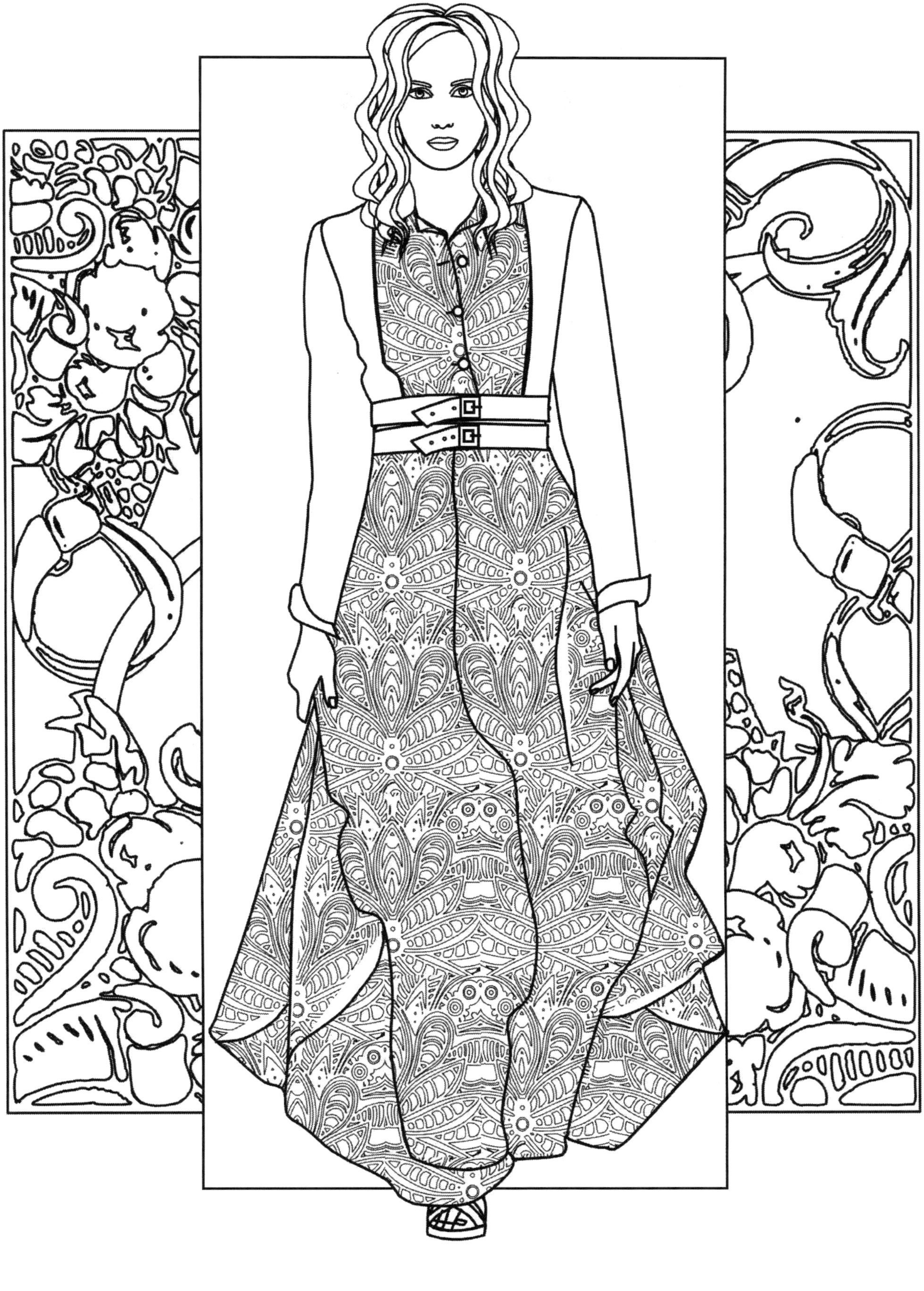

FASHION NOTES

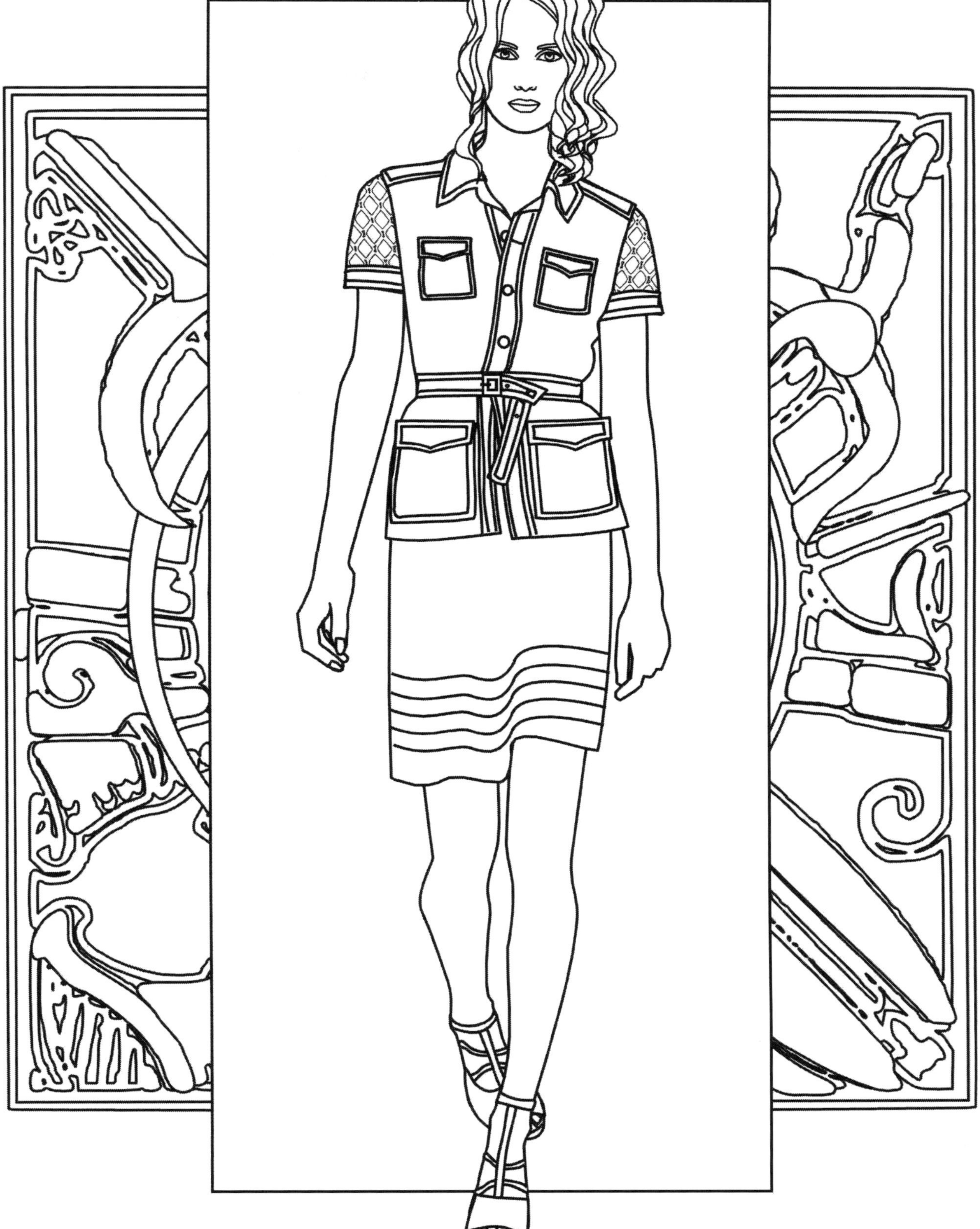

FASHION NOTES

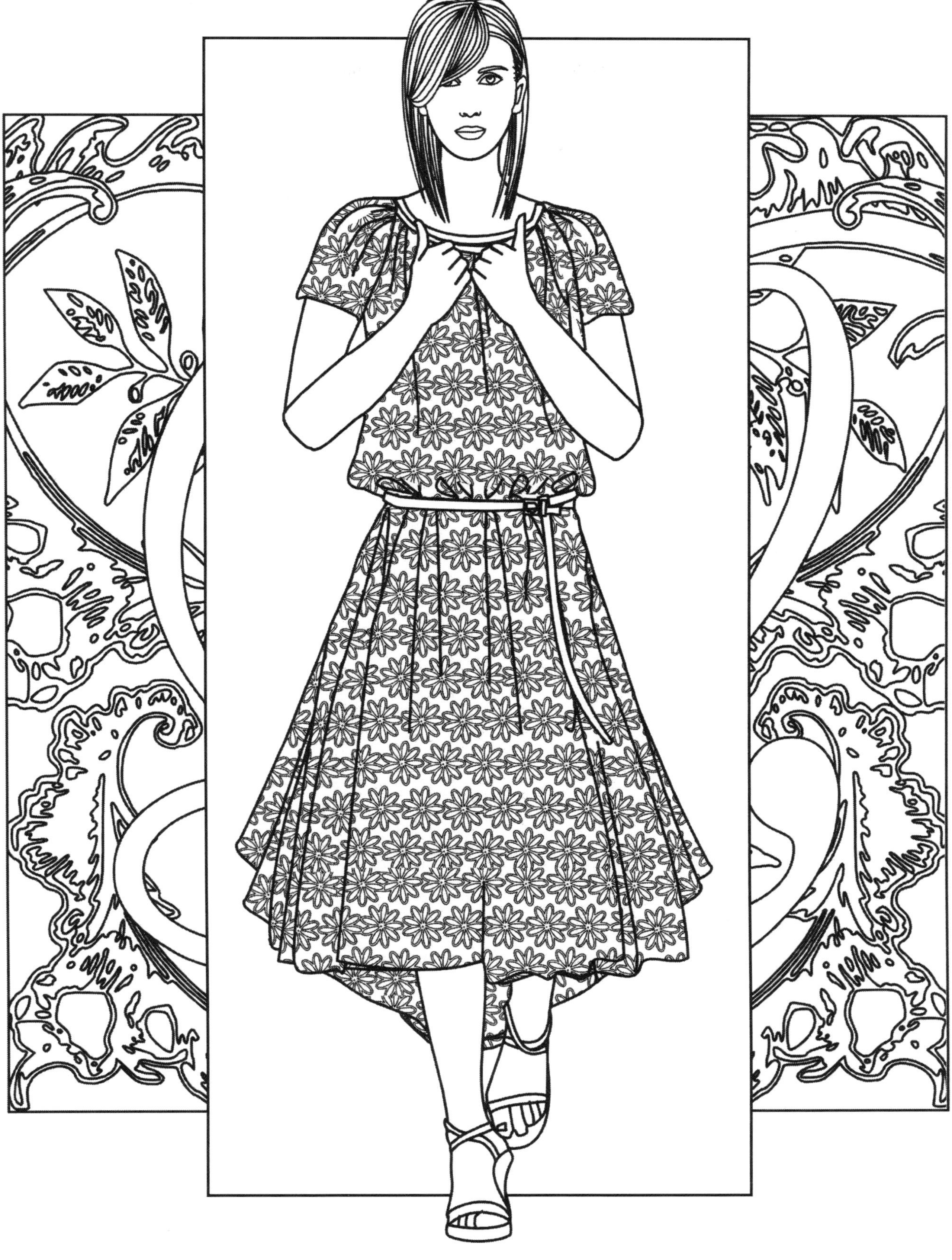

FASHION NOTES

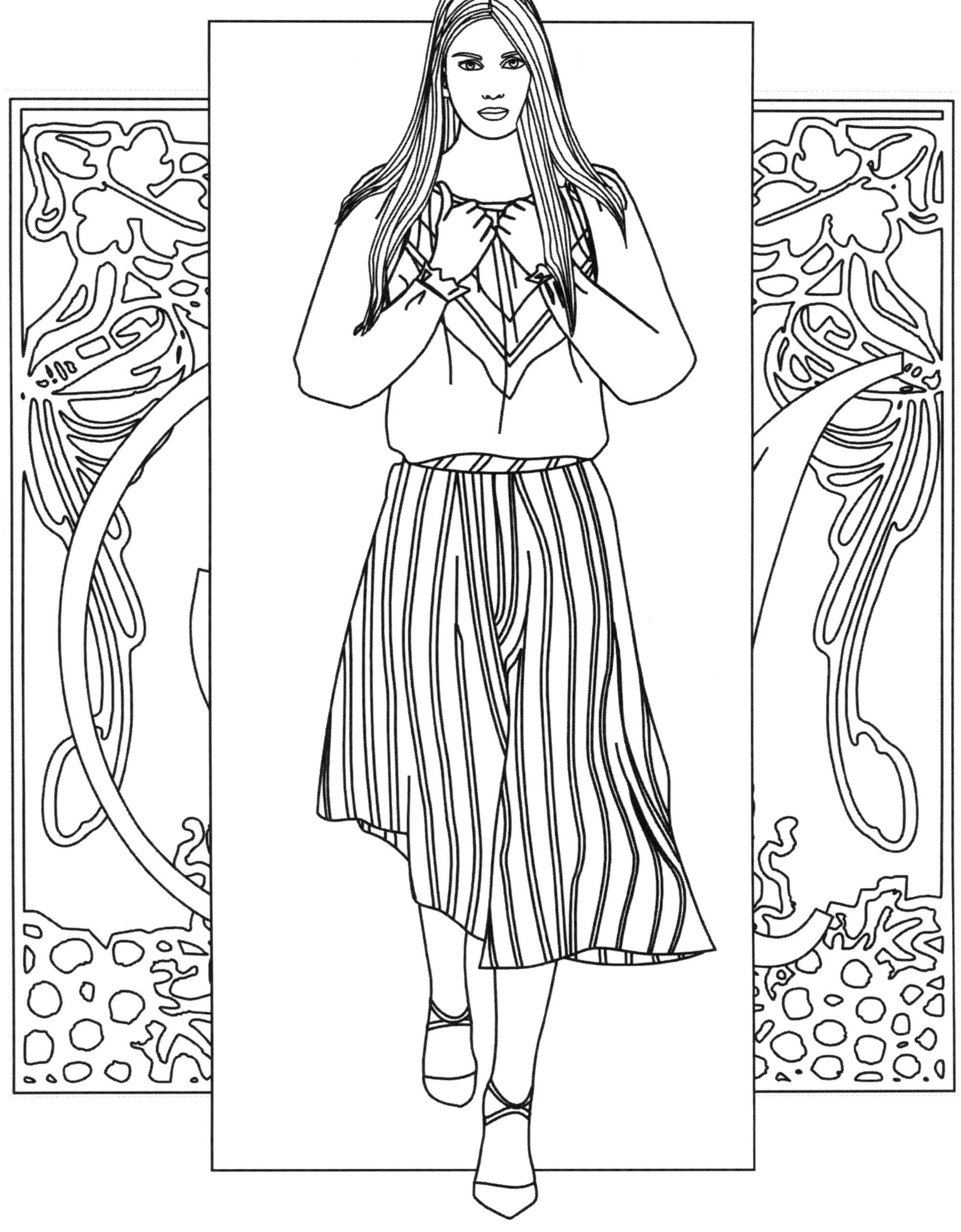

FASHION NOTES

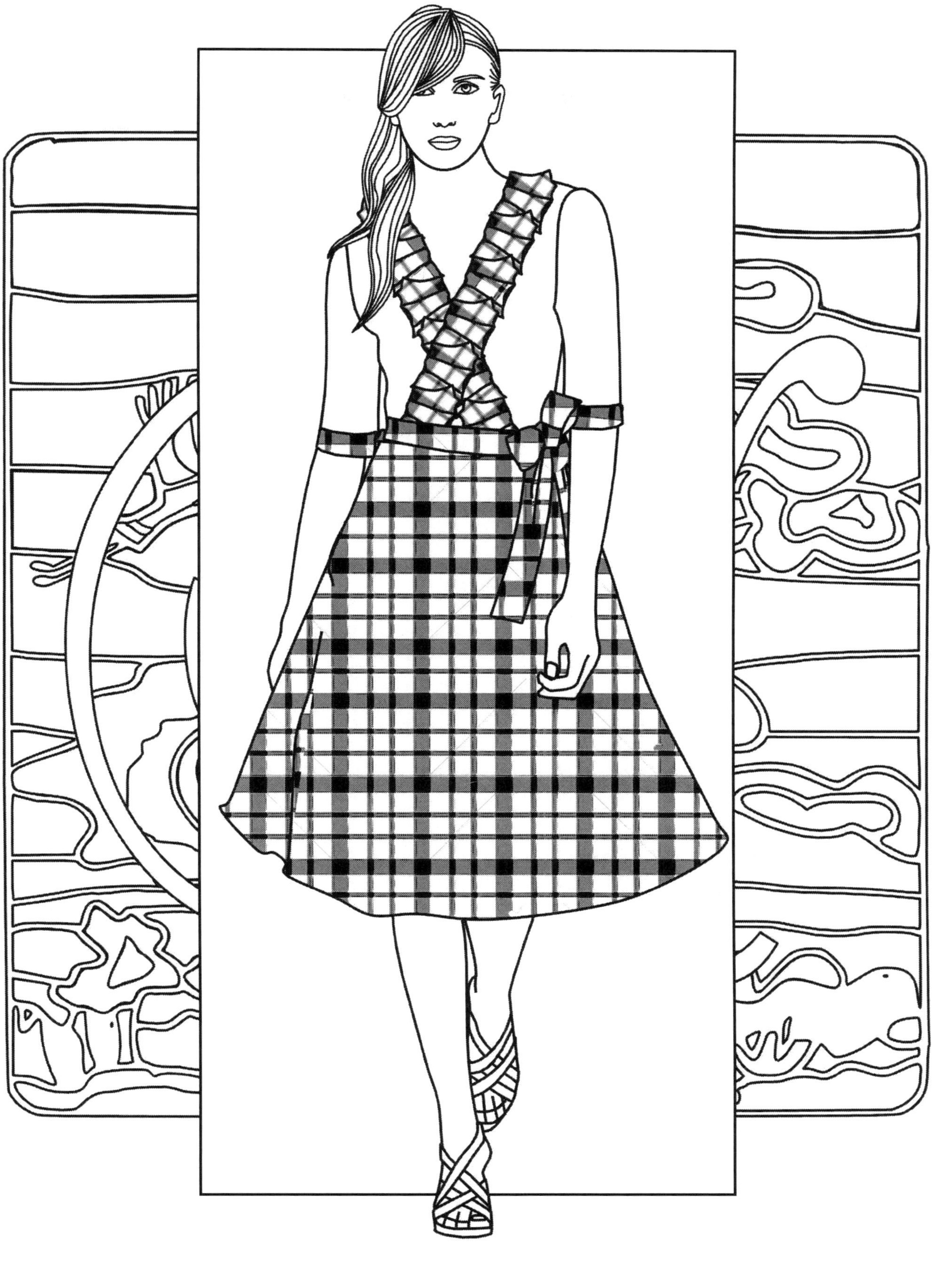

FASHION NOTES

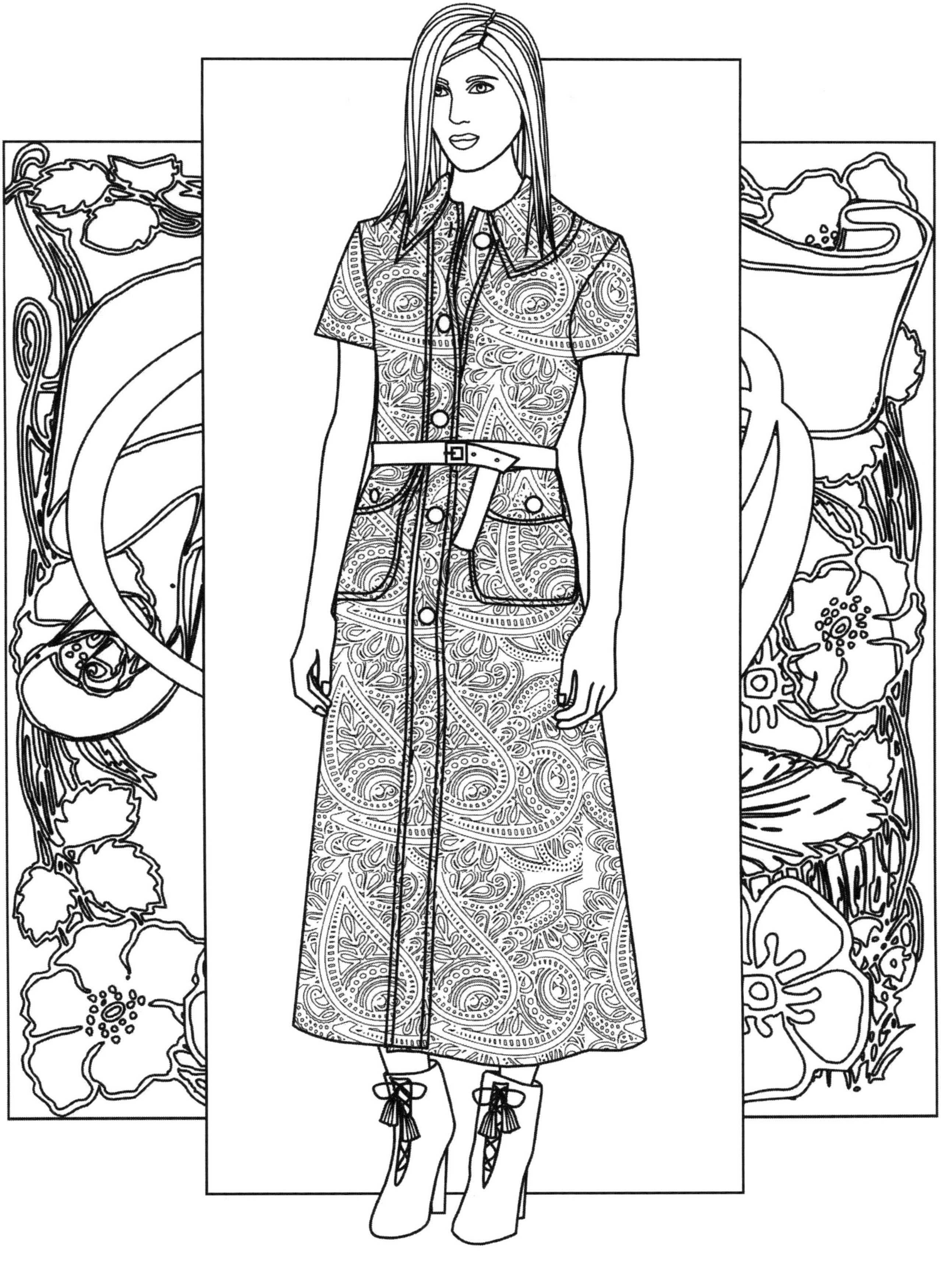

FASHION NOTES

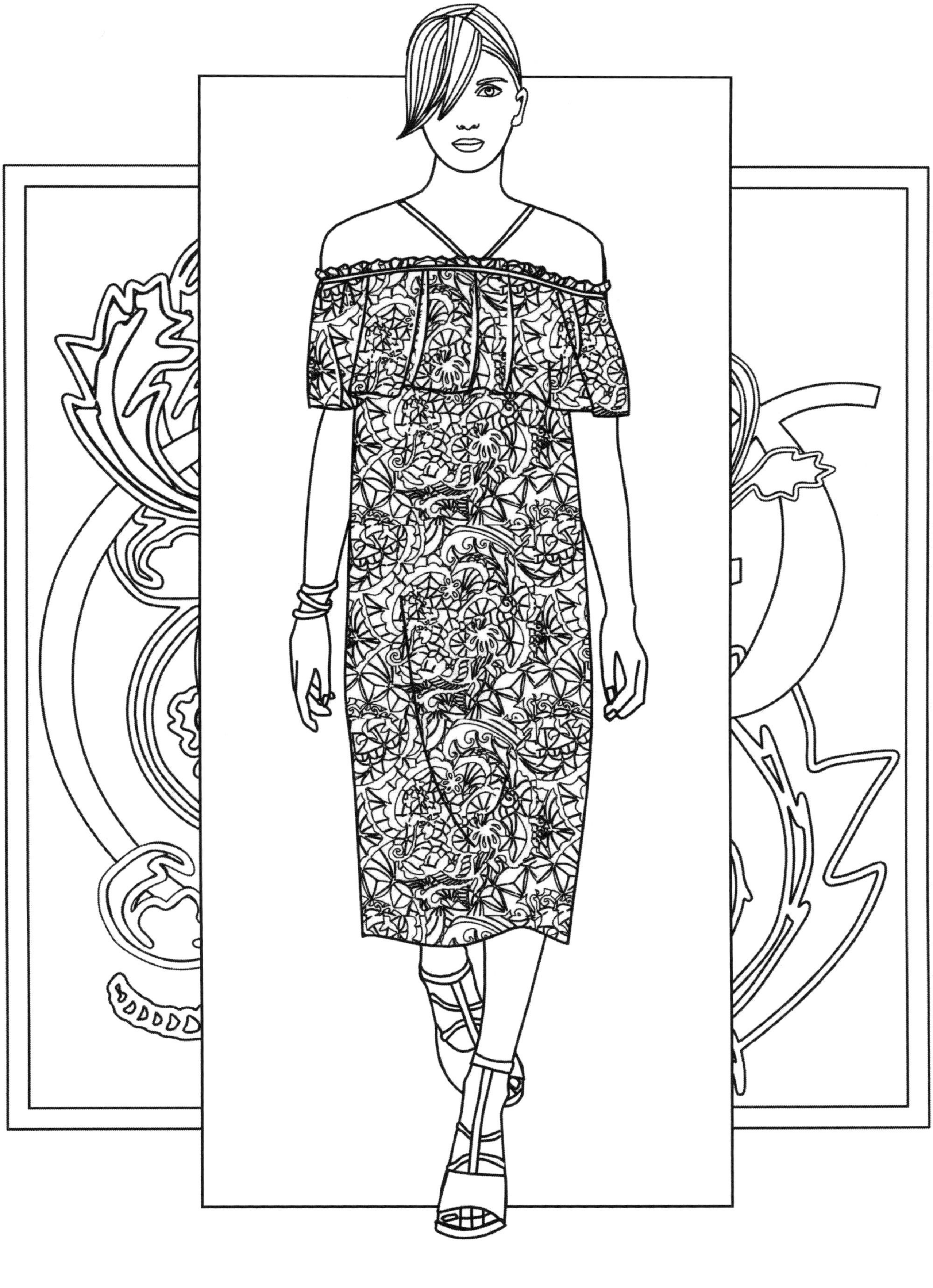

FASHION NOTES

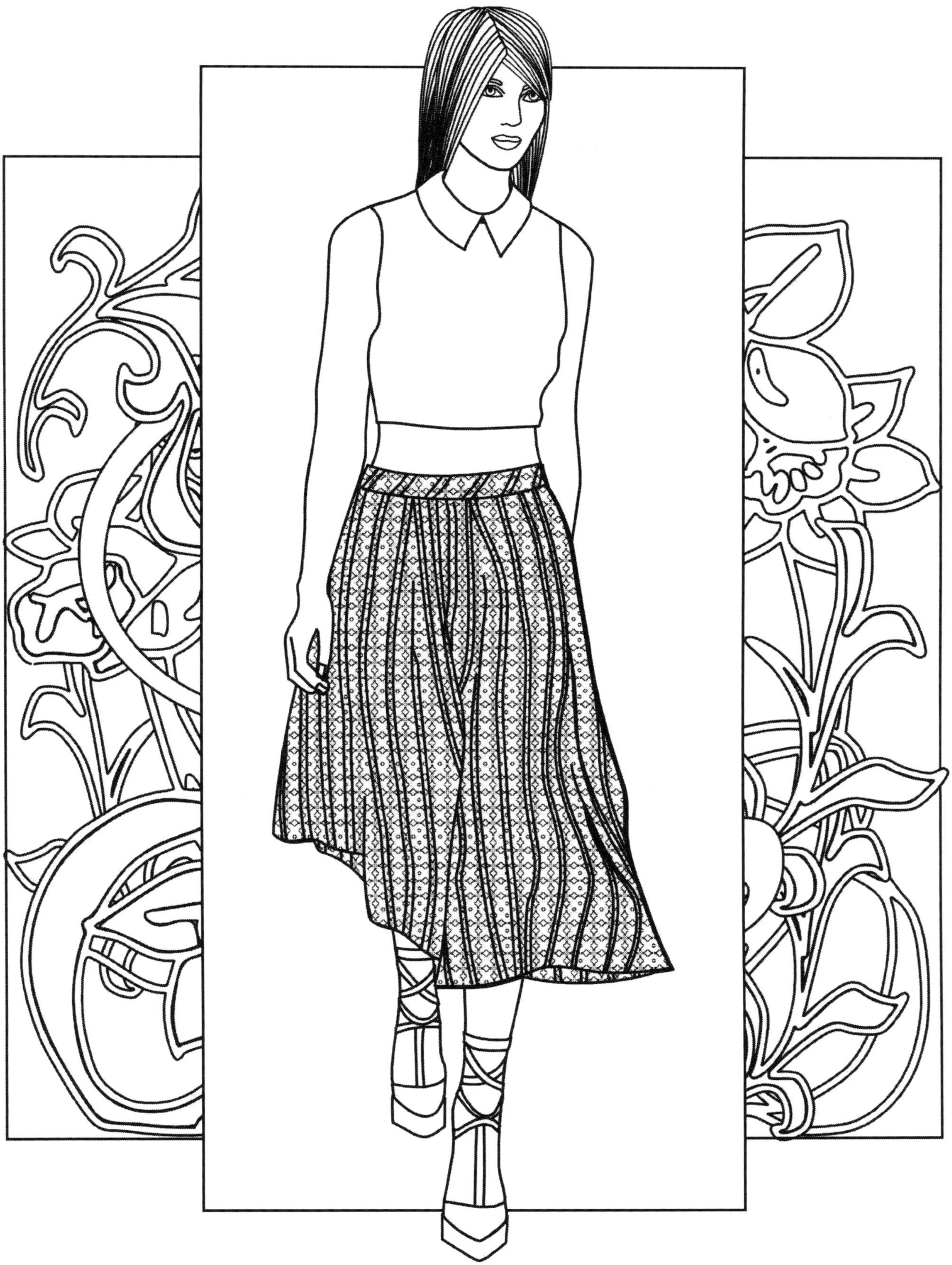

FASHION NOTES

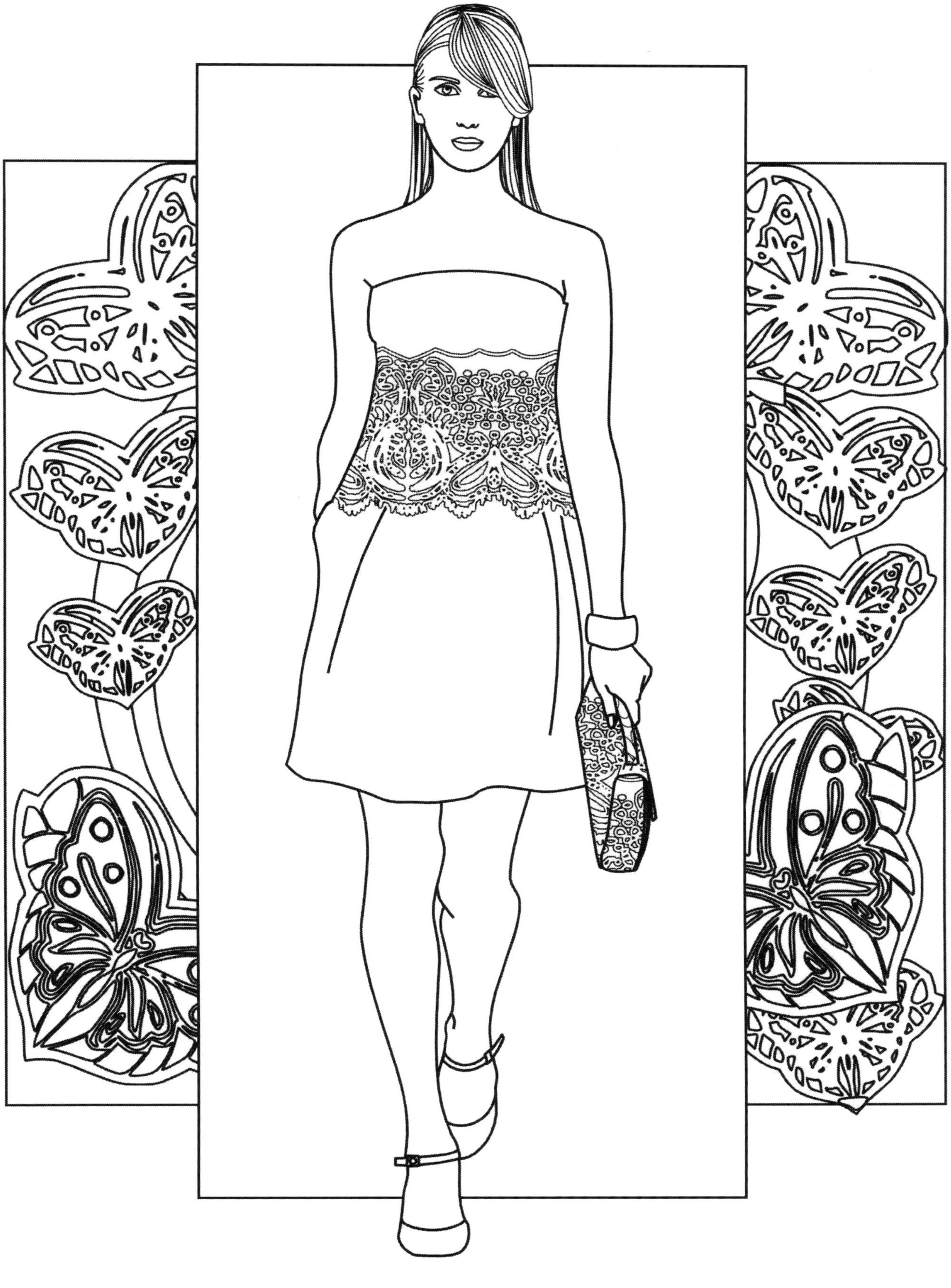

FASHION NOTES

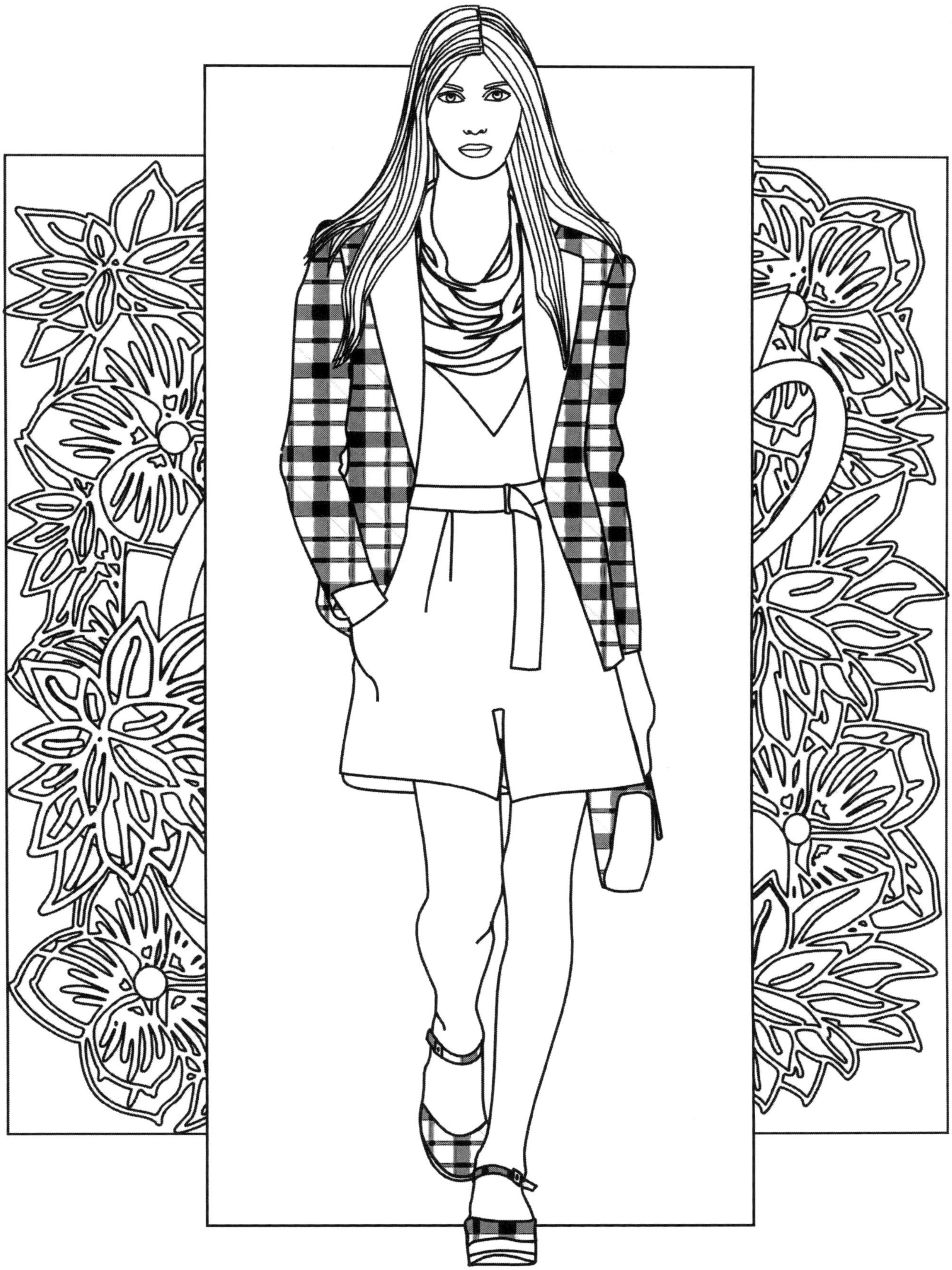

FASHION NOTES

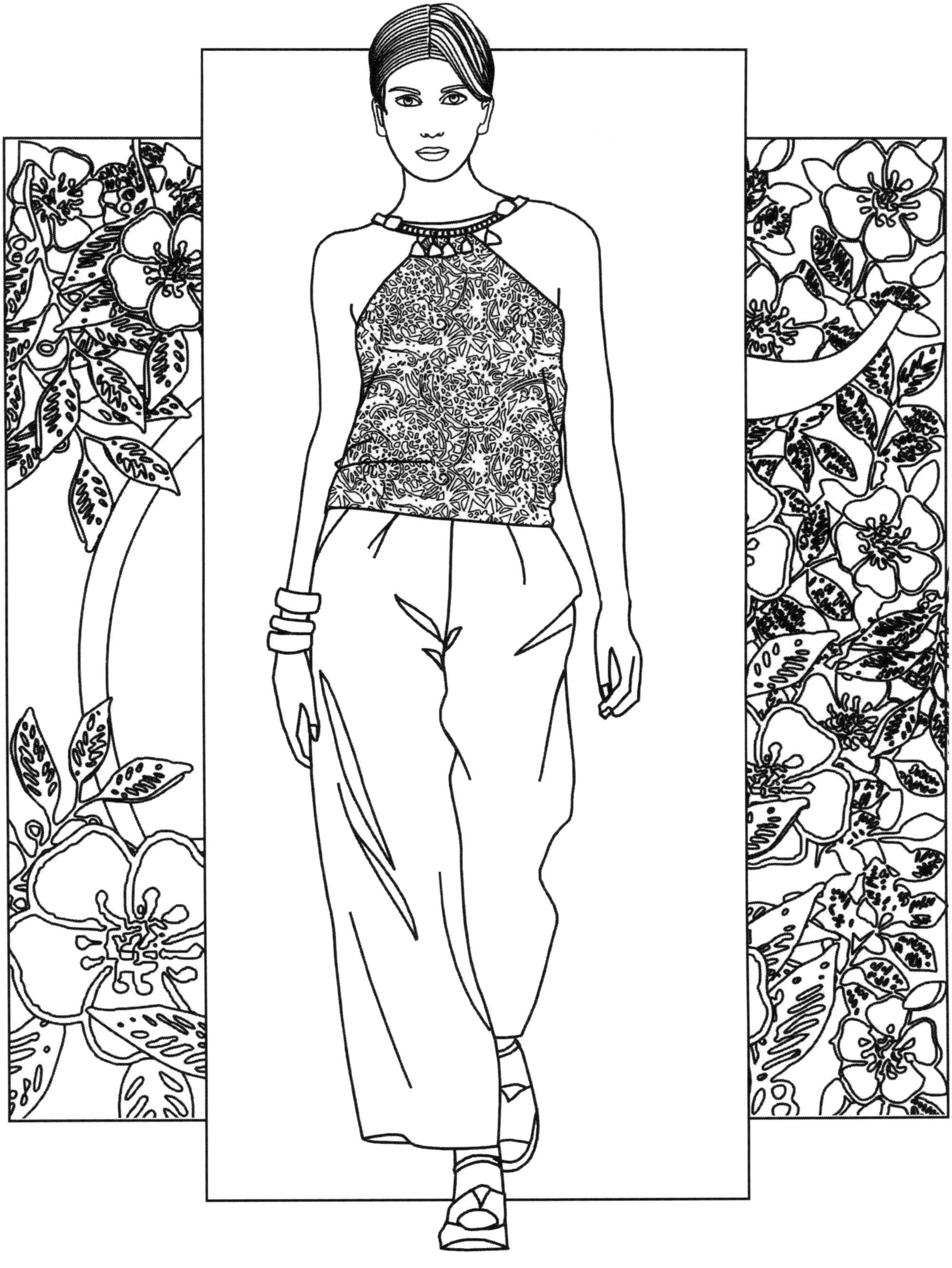

FASHION NOTES

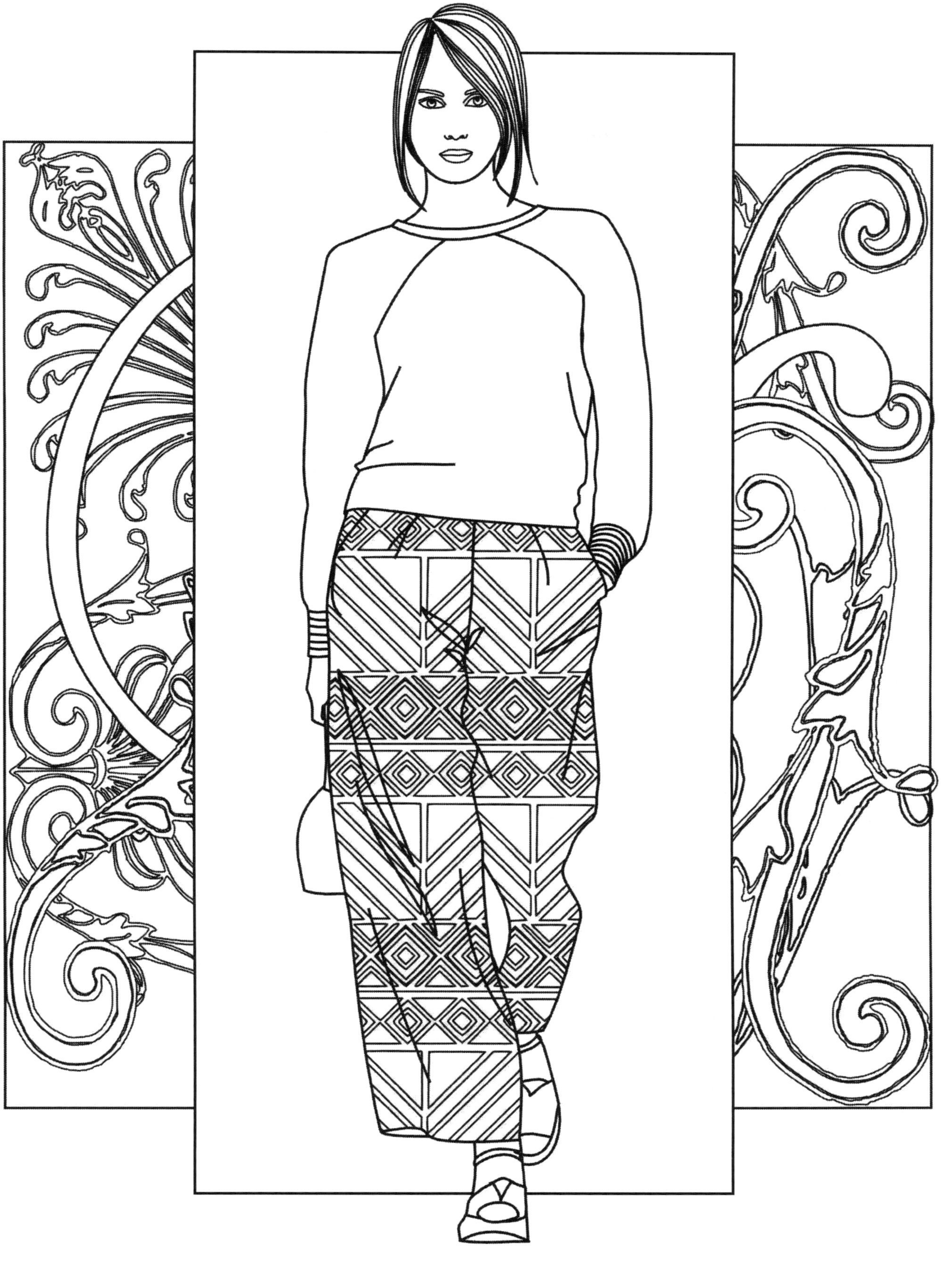

FASHION NOTES

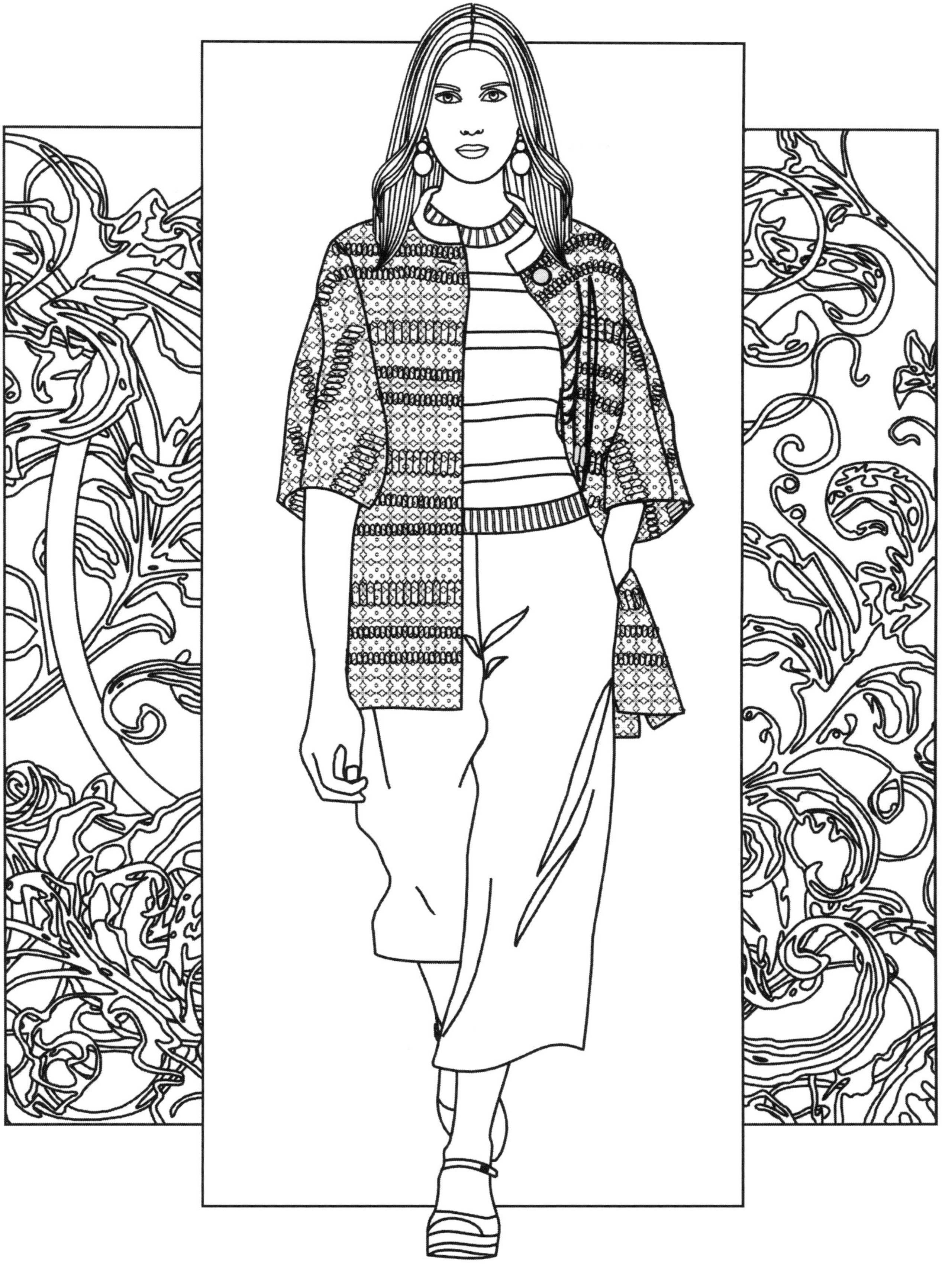

FASHION NOTES

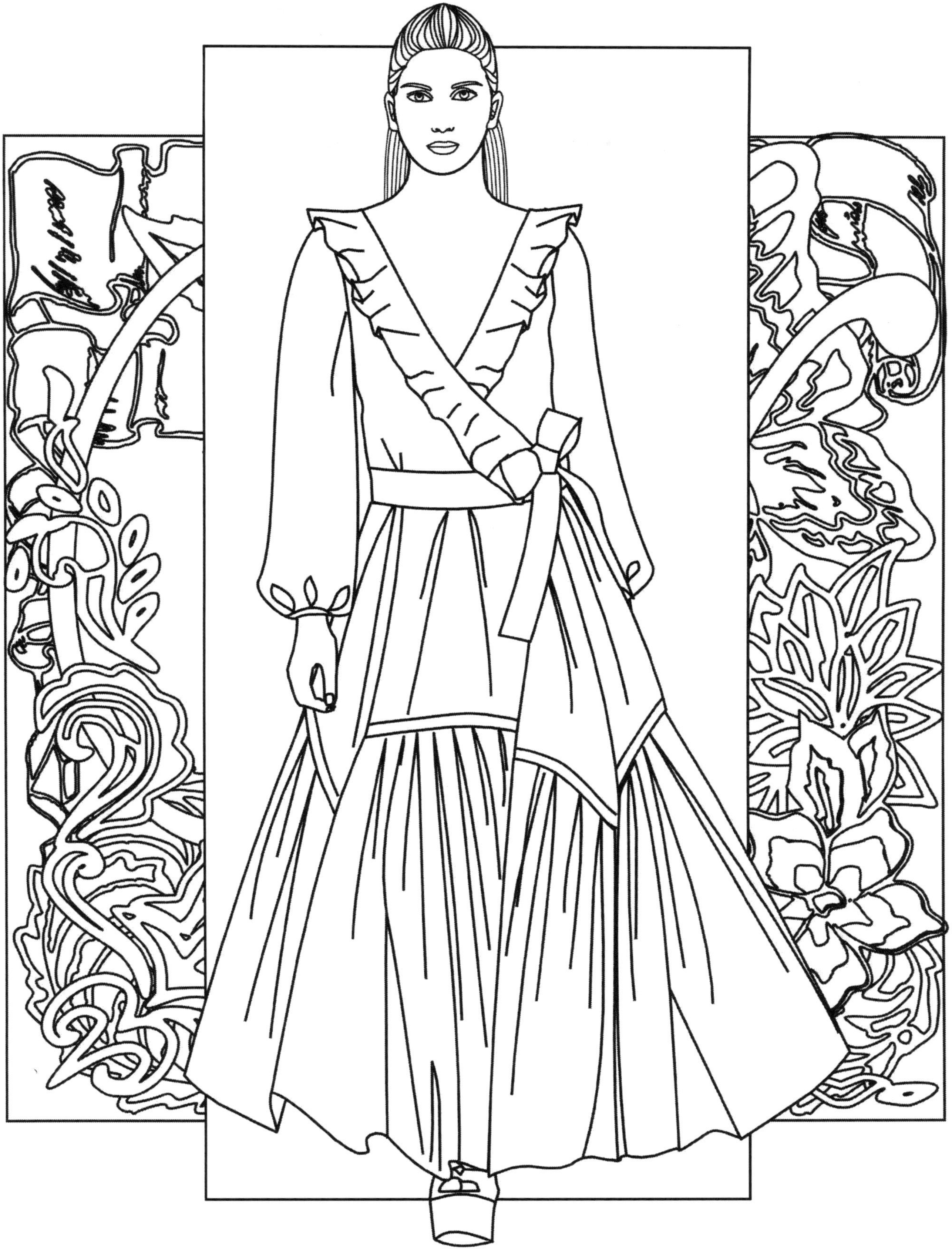

FASHION NOTES

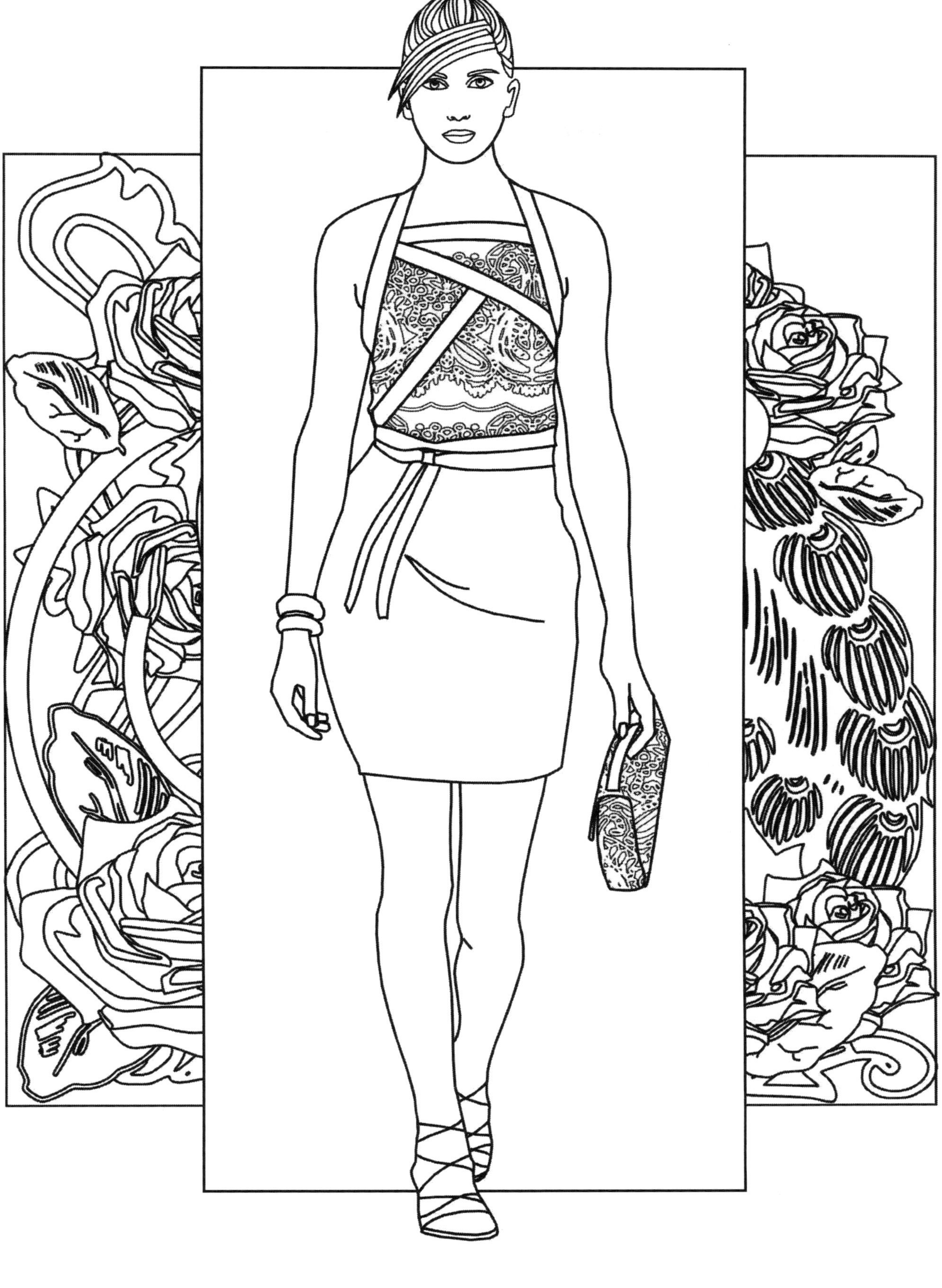

FASHION NOTES

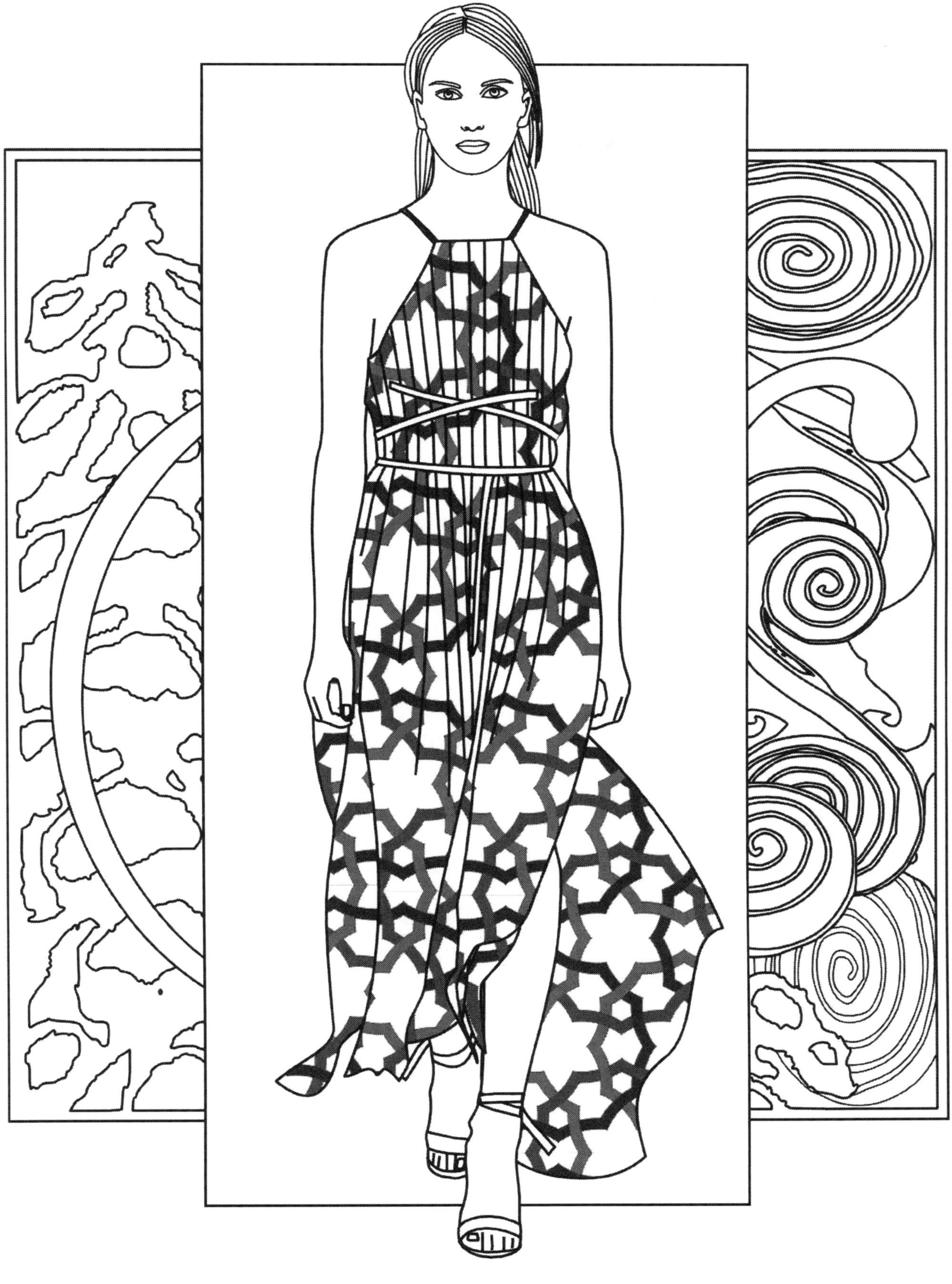

FASHION NOTES

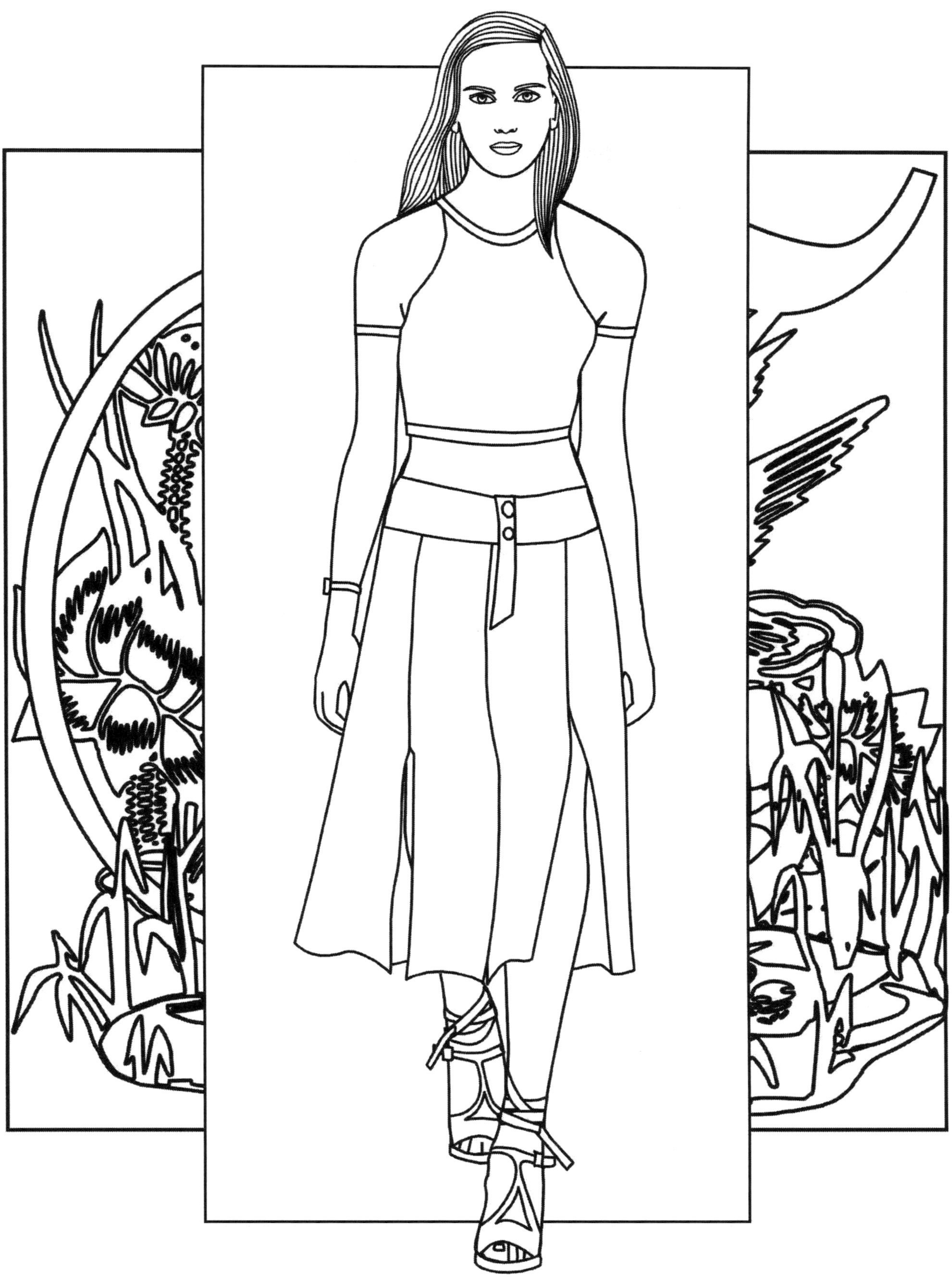

FASHION NOTES

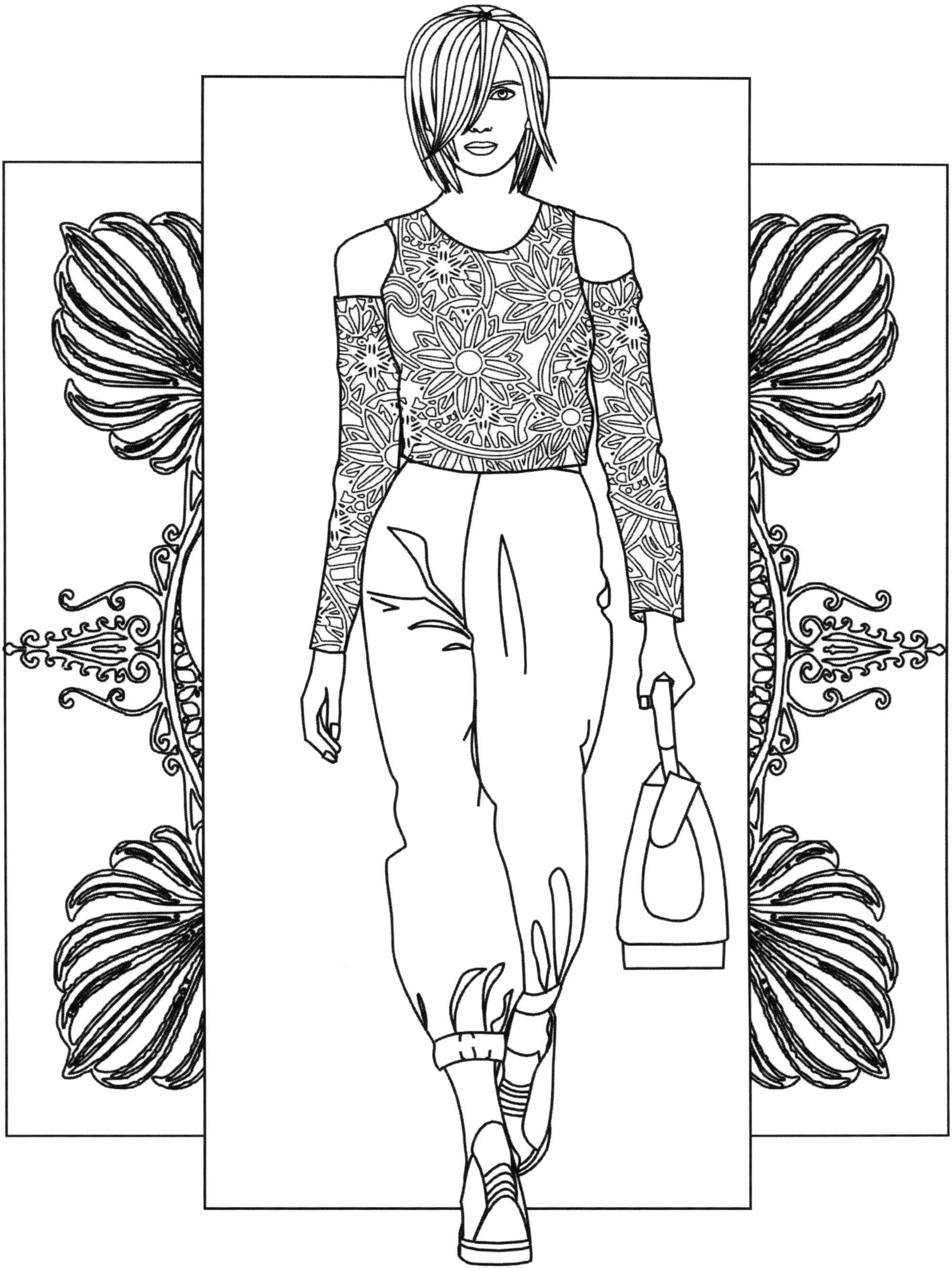

FASHION NOTES

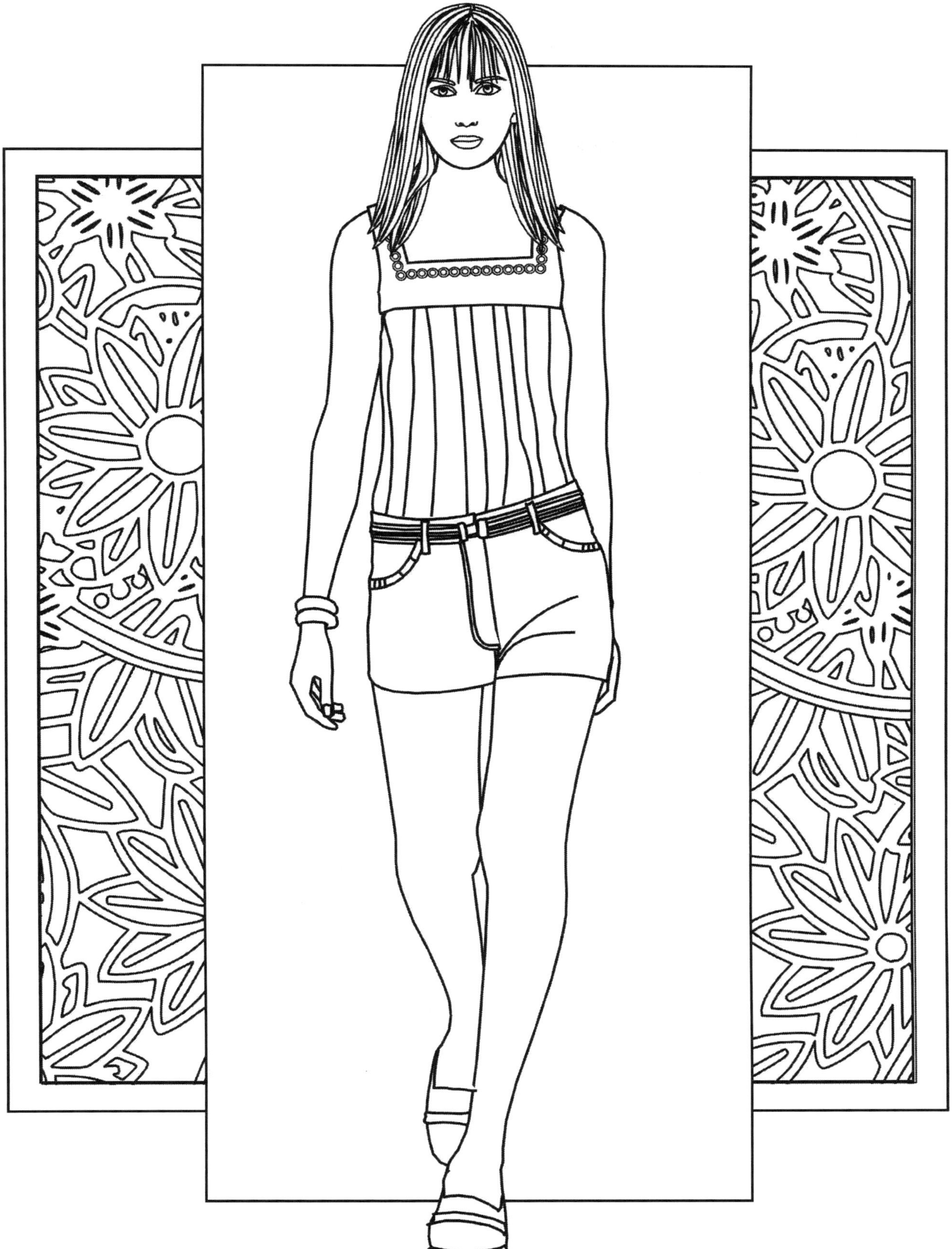

FASHION NOTES

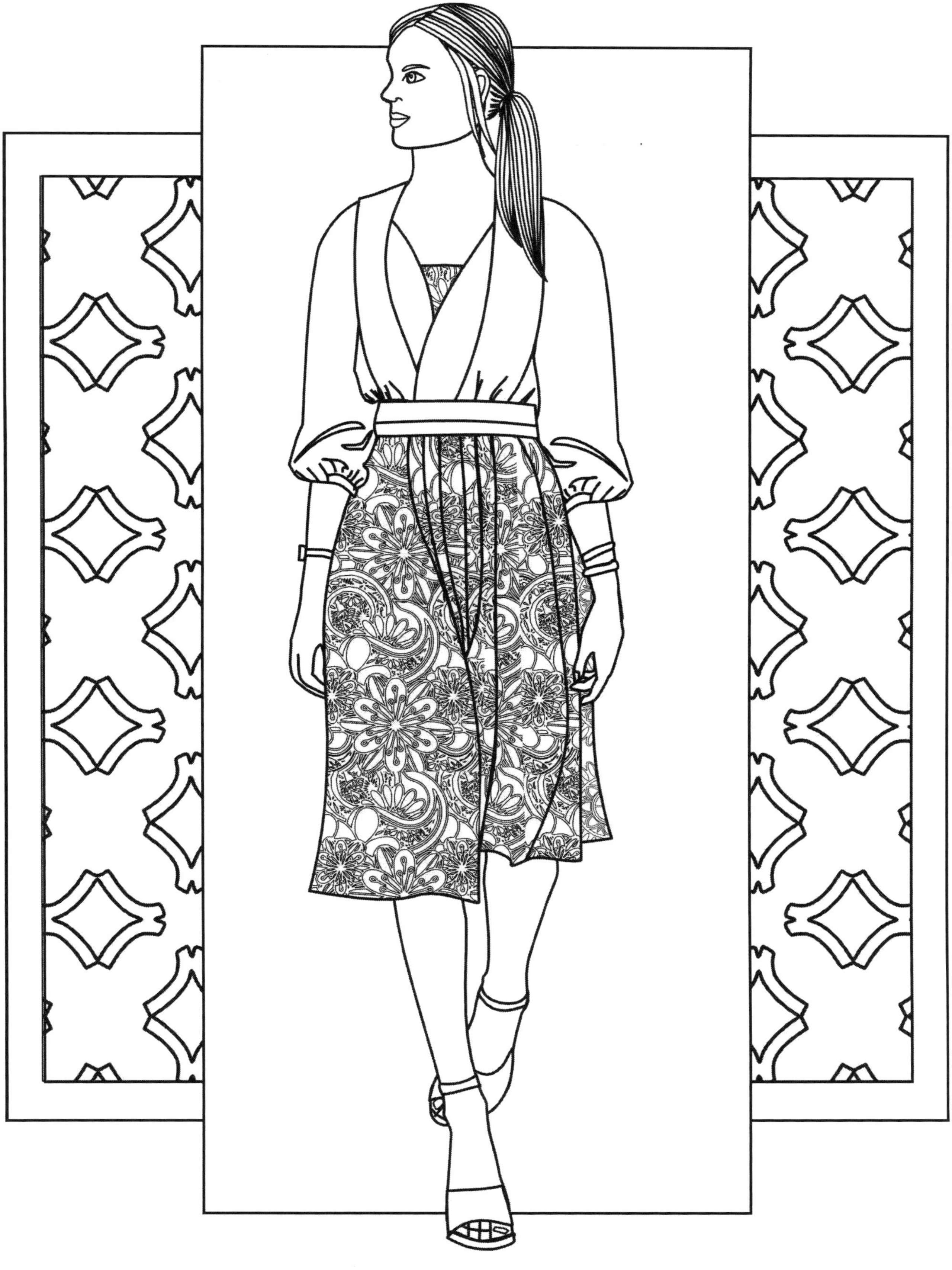

FASHION NOTES

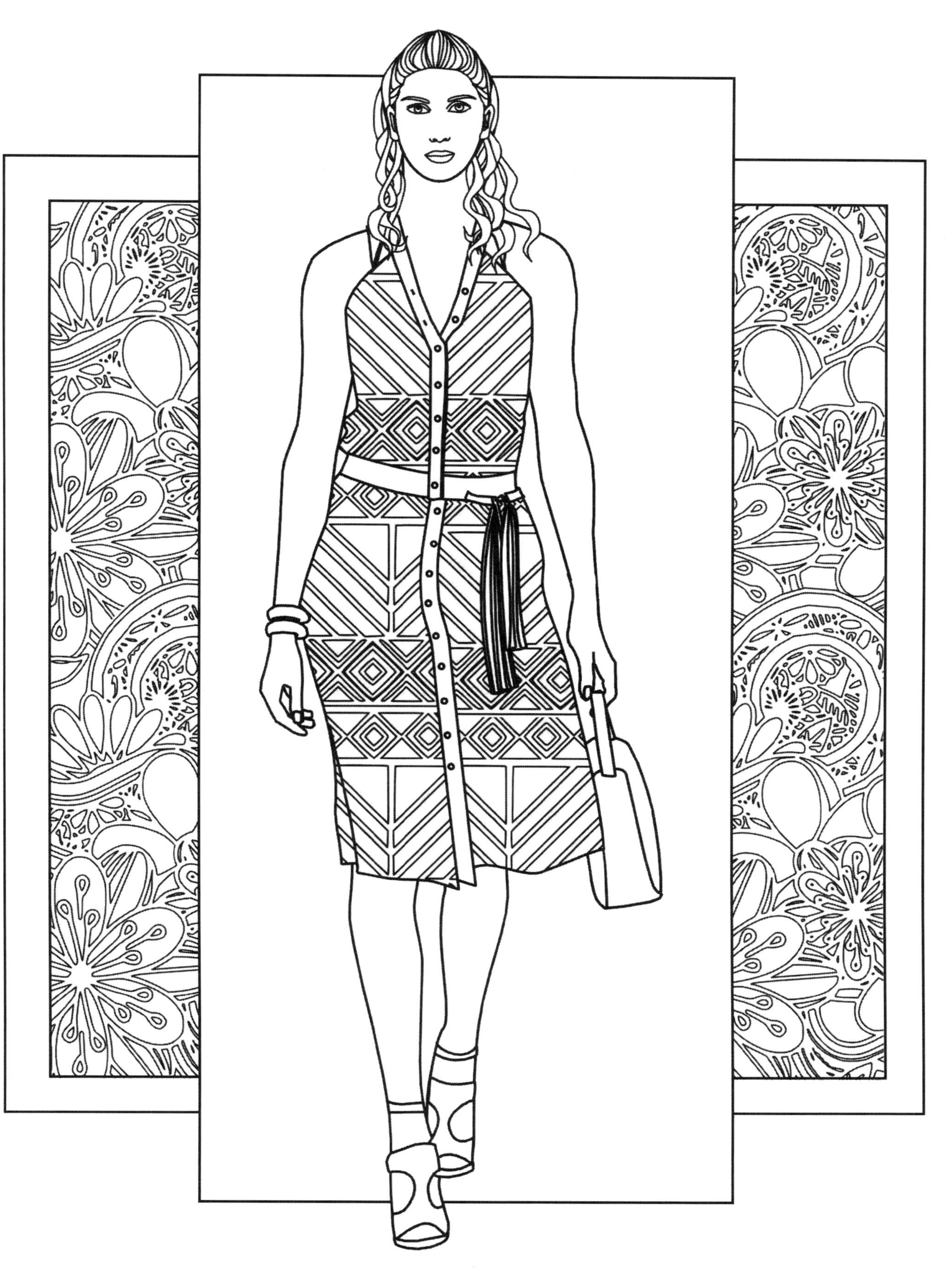

FASHION NOTES

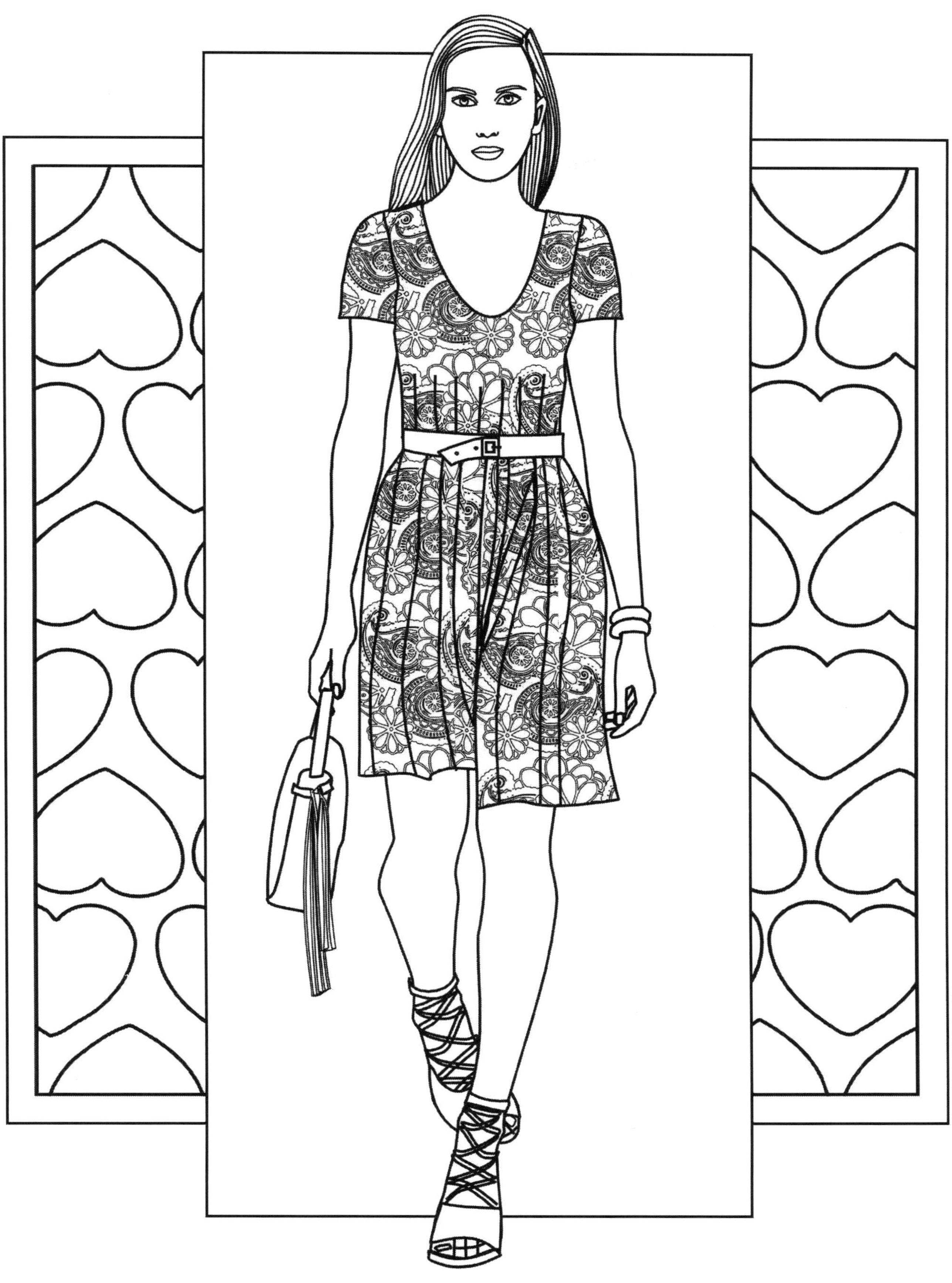

FASHION NOTES

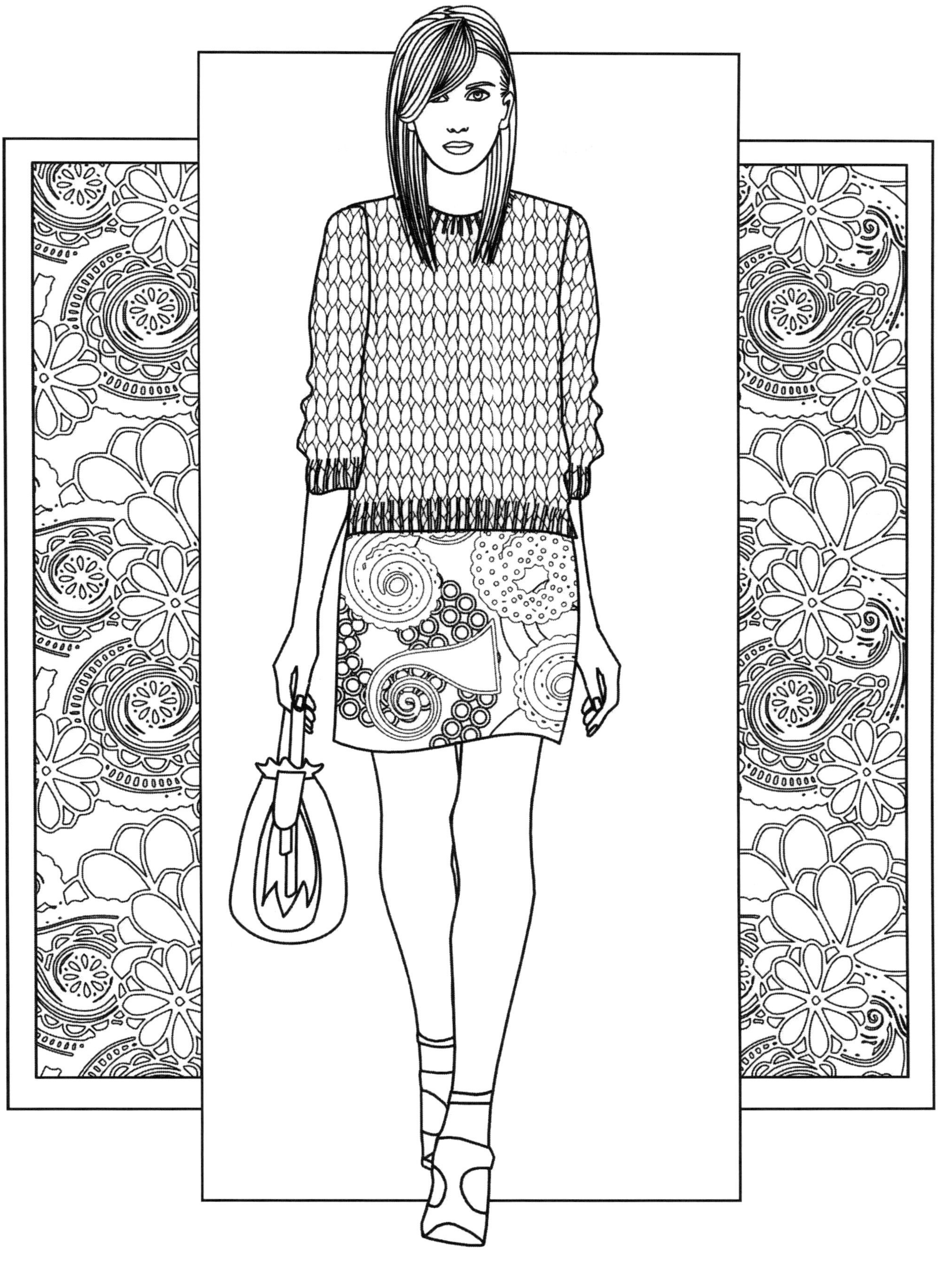

FASHION NOTES

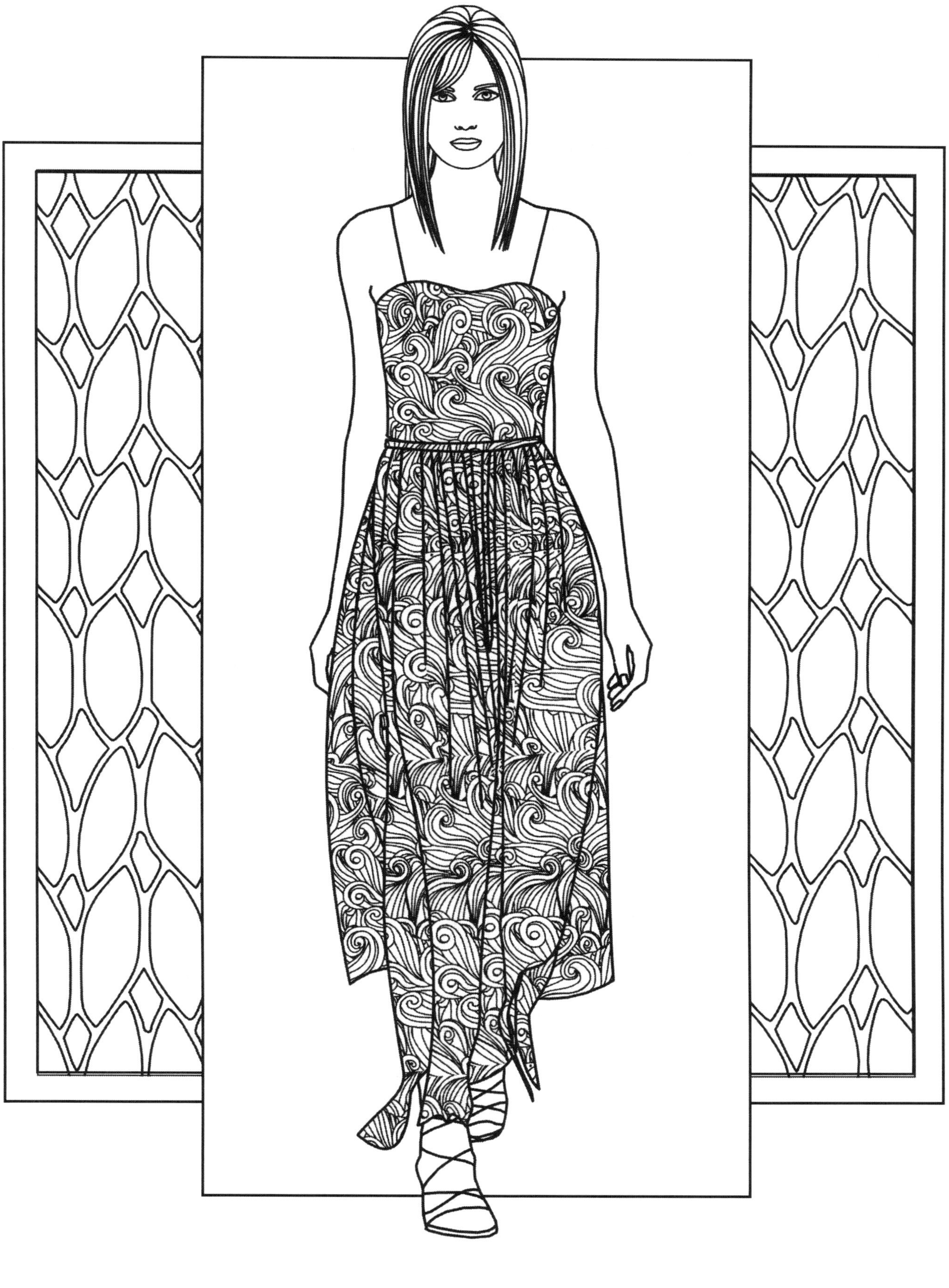

FASHION NOTES

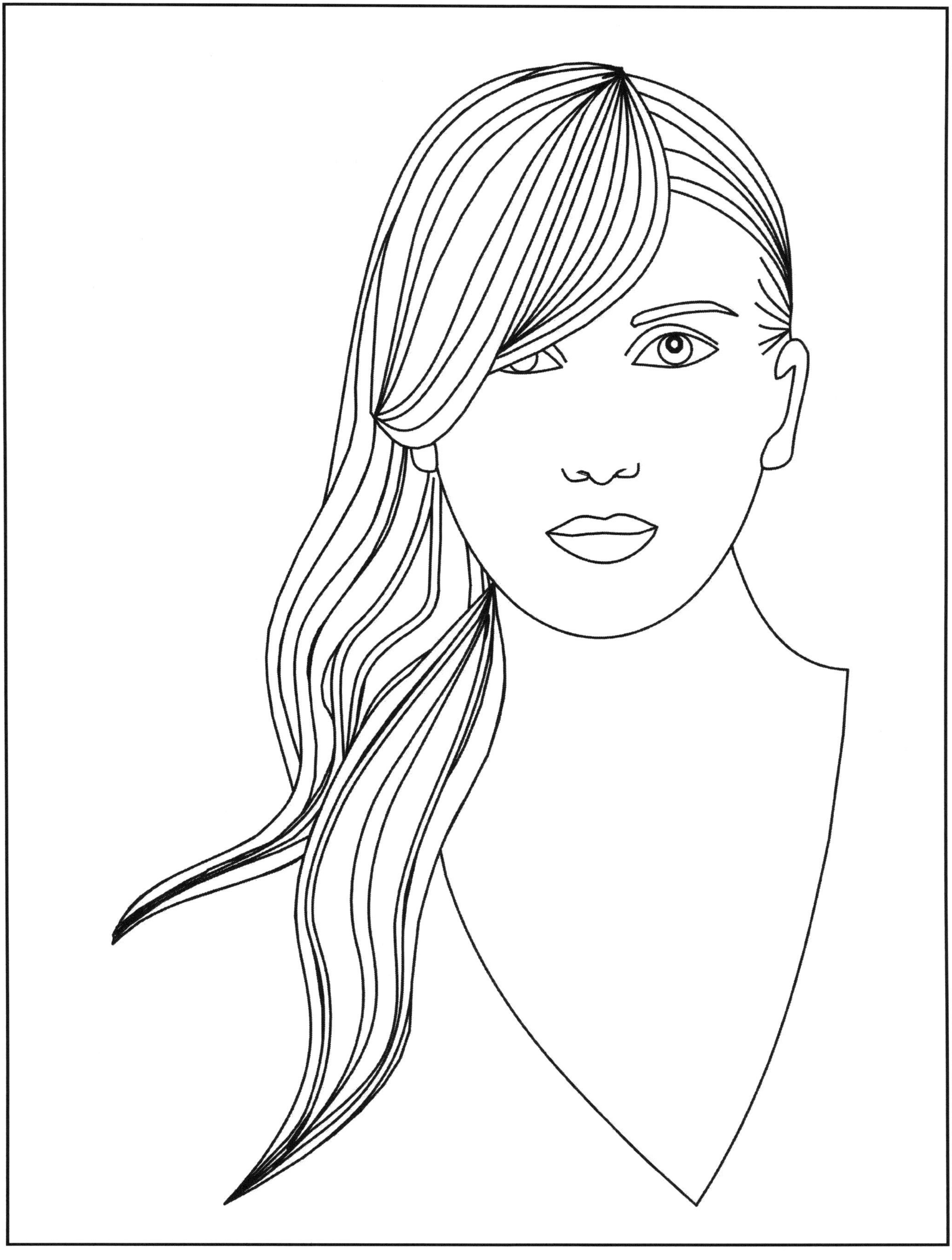

FASHION NOTES

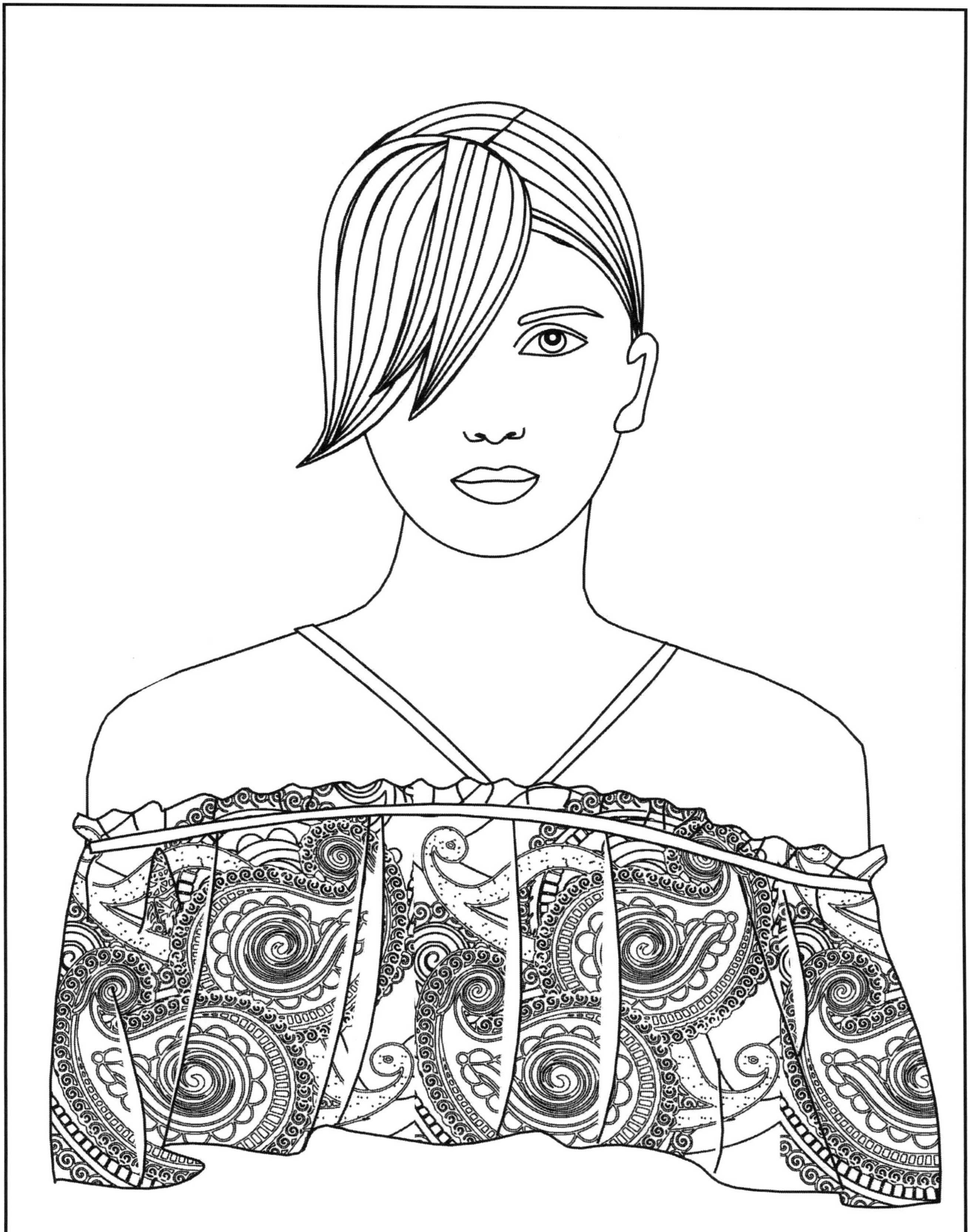

FASHION NOTES

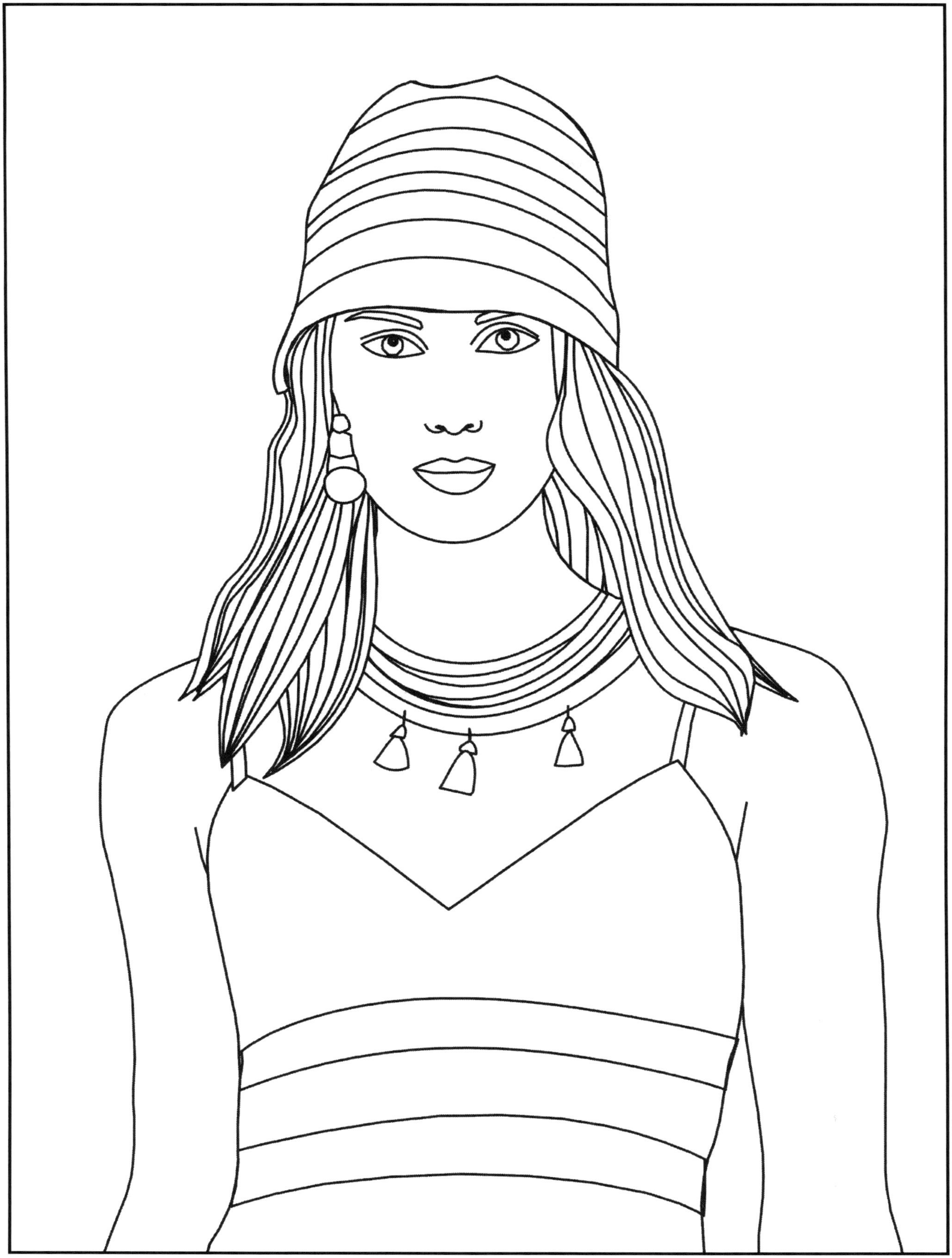

LISE
Publishing

Printed in Great Britain
by Amazon